THE POWER OF PRAYER

Charles Spurgeon

GLH Publishing
LOUISVILLE, KY

Compiled from sermons 1091, 672, 700, 1018, 1024, and 1390 of
   Charles Spurgeon.

This work has been lightly edited to update include footnotes
   to aid the reader.

ISBN:
   Paperback 978-1-941129-79-1

CONTENTS

I. Prayer Certain of Success 1

II. The Ravens' Cry 16

III. Order and Argument in Prayer 32

IV. Pleading 49

V. The Throne of Grace 64

VI. Brief, Silent Prayer 80

I. Prayer Certain of Success

And I say unto you, ask, and it shall be given you;
seek, and you shall find; knock, and it shall be opened
unto you. For everyone that asks receives and he that
seeks finds; and to him that knocks it shall be opened
Luke 11:9-10.

To seek aid in time of distress from a supernatural being is an instinct of human nature. We say not that human nature unrenewed ever offers truly spiritual prayer, or ever exercises saving faith in the living God. But still, like a child crying in the dark with painful longing for help from somewhere or other, it scarcely knows where, the soul in deep sorrow almost invariably cries to some supernatural being for succor. None have been more ready to pray in time of trouble than those who have ridiculed prayer in their prosperity—and probably no prayers have been more true to the feelings of the hour than those which atheists have offered under the pressure of the fear of death.

In one of his papers in the *Tattler*, Addison describes a man, who, on board ship, loudly boasted of his atheism. A brisk gale springing up, he fell upon his knees and confessed to the chaplain that he had been an atheist. The common seamen who had never heard the word before, thought it had been some strange fish, but were more surprised when they saw it was a man and learned out of his own mouth, "that he never believed till that day that there was a God." One of the old sailors whispered to the boatswain that it would be a good deed to heave him overboard, but this was a cruel suggestion, for the poor creature was already in misery enough—his atheism had evaporated and he, in mortal terror, cried to God to have mercy upon him!

Similar incidents have occurred, not once nor twice. Indeed, so frequently does boastful skepticism come down with a run at the last that we always expect it to do so. Take away unnatural restraint from the mind and it may be said of all men that, like the comrades of Jonah,

1

they cry, every man, unto his God in their trouble. As birds
to their nests, hinds to their coverts,[1] so men in agony fly
to a superior being for succor in the hour of need. God has
given to all the creatures He has made some peculiar form
of strength—one has such swiftness of foot that at the bay-
ing of a hound it escapes from danger by outstripping the
wind. Another, with outspread wings, is lifted beyond the
fowler. A third, with horns, pushes down its enemy and a
fourth, with tooth and claw, tears in pieces its adversary.

To man He gave but little strength compared with the
animals among which He placed in Eden and yet man was
king over all because the Lord was His strength. So long
as he knew where to look for the source of his power, man
remained the unresisted monarch of all around him. That
image of God in which he shone resplendent sustained his
sovereignty over the fowls of the air, the beasts of the field
and the fish of the sea. By instinct man turned to his God
in Paradise and now, though he is, to a sad degree, an un-
crowned monarch, there lingers in his memory shadows
of what he was and remembrances of where his strength
must still be found. Therefore, no matter where you find
a man, you meet one who, in his distress, will ask for supernatural help.

I believe in the truthfulness of this instinct and that
man prays because there is something in prayer. And
when the Creator gives His creature the power of thirst, it
is because water exists to meet its thirst—and as when He
creates hunger there is food to correspond to the appetite.
So when He inclines men to pray it is because prayer has a
corresponding blessing connected with it. We find a powerful reason for expecting prayer to be effectual in the fact
that it is an institution of God. In God's Word we are over
and over again commanded to pray. God's institutions are
not folly. Can I believe that the infinitely wise God has ordained for me an exercise which is ineffectual and is no
more than child's play?

Does He bid me pray and yet has prayer no more result than if I whistled to the wind, or sang to a grove of
trees? If there is no answer to prayer, prayer is a monstrous
absurdity and God is the Author of it—which it is blasphemy to assert! No man who is not a fool will continue to
pray when you have once proved to him that prayer has
no effect with God and never receives an answer. Prayer is
a work for idiots and madmen, and not for sane persons,

---

1   Deer to their hiding places.

if it is, indeed, true, that its effects end with the man who prays! I shall not, this morning, enter into any arguments upon the matter—rather, I am coming to my text, which to me, at least, and to you who are followers of Christ, is the end of all controversy.

Our Savior knew right well that many difficulties would arise in connection with prayer which might tend to stagger His disciples and therefore He has balanced every opposition by an overwhelming assurance. Read those words, "I say unto you," I—your Teacher, your Master, your Lord, your Savior, your God—"I say unto you, ask, and it shall be given you; seek, and you shall find; knock, and it shall be opened unto you." In the text our Lord meets all difficulties—first by giving us the weight of His own authority, "I say unto you." Next by presenting us with a promise, "Ask, and it shall be given you," and so on. And then by reminding us of an indisputable fact—"everyone that asks receives." Here are three mortal wounds for a Christian's doubts as to prayer.

I. First, then, our Savior gives to us the weight of his own authority, "I say unto you." The first mark of a follower of Christ is that he believes his Lord. We do not follow the Lord at all if we raise any questions upon points whereupon He speaks positively. Though a doctrine should be surrounded with 10,000 difficulties, the *ipse dixit*[2] of the Lord Jesus sweeps them all away, so far as true Christians are concerned. Our Master's declaration is all the argument we need. "I say unto you," is our logic. Reason? We see you at your best in Jesus, for He is made of God unto us Wisdom. He cannot err, He cannot lie and if He says, "I say unto you," that is the end of all debate.

But, brothers and sisters, there are certain reasons which should lead us the more confidently to rest in our Master's Word upon this point. There is power in every Word of the Lord Jesus, but there is special force in the utterance before us. It has been objected to prayer that it is not possible that it should be answered because the laws of nature are unalterable and they must and will go on whether men pray or not. Not a drop of water will change its position in a single wave, or a particle of infectious matter be turned from its course though all the saints in the universe should plead against tempest and plague.

Now, concerning that matter, we are in no hurry to make an answer—our adversaries have more to prove

---

2   A dogmatic and unproven statement.

than we have—and among the rest they have to prove a
negative. To us it does not seem necessary to prove that
the laws of nature are disturbed. God can work miracles
and He may work them yet again as He has done in days
of yore, but it is no part of the Christian faith that God
must work miracles in order to answer the prayers of His
servants. When a man, in order to fulfill a promise, has
to disarrange all his affairs and, so to speak, to stop all
his machinery, it proves that he is but a man and that his
wisdom and power are limited. But He is God, indeed,
who, without reversing the engine or removing a single
cog from a wheel, fulfills the desires of His people as they
come up before Him!

The Lord is so omnipotent that He can work results
tantamount to miracles without, in the slightest degree,
suspending any of His laws. He did, as it were, in the old-
en times, stop the machinery of the universe to answer
prayer, but now, with equally godlike glory, He orders
events so as to answer believing prayers and yet suspends
no natural law. But this is far from being our only or our
main comfort—that lies in the fact that we hear the voice
of One who is competent to speak upon the matter and
He says, "I say unto you, ask and it shall be given you."
Whether the laws of nature are reversible or irreversible,
"Ask and it shall be given you; seek, and you shall find."

Now, who is He that speaks thus? It is he that made
all things, without whom was not anything made that was
made! Cannot He speak to this point? O You eternal Word,
You who were in the beginning with God, balancing the
clouds and fastening the foundations of the earth, You
know what the laws and the unalterable constitutions of
nature may be and if you say, "Ask and it shall be given
you," then assuredly it will be so, be the laws of nature
what they may! Besides, our Lord is by us adored as the
Sustainer of all things and, seeing that all the laws of nature are only operative through His power and are sustained in their motion by His might, He must be cognizant
of the motion of all the forces in the world—and if He says,
"Ask and it shall be given you"—He does not speak in ig-
norance, but knows what He affirms. We may be assured
that there are no forces which can prevent the fulfillment
of the Lord's own Word. From the Creator and the Sustainer the Words, "I say unto you," settles all controversy
forever.

But another objection has been raised which is very

ancient, indeed, and has a great appearance of force. It is raised not so much by skeptics, as by those who hold a part of the Truth. It is this—that prayer can certainly produce no result because the decrees of God have settled everything and those decrees are Immutable. Now we have no desire to deny the assertion that the decrees of God have settled all events. It is our full belief that God has foreknown and predestinated everything that happens in Heaven above or in the earth beneath—and that the foreknown station of a reed by the river is as fixed as the station of a king—and "the chaff from the hand of the winnower is steered as the stars in their courses." Predestination embraces the great and the little, and reaches unto all things—the question is, why do we pray?

Might it not as logically be asked why we breathe, eat, move, or do anything? We have an answer which satisfies us, namely, that our prayers are in the predestination and that God has as much ordained His people's prayers as anything else. And when we pray we are producing links in the chain of ordained facts! Destiny decrees that I should pray—I pray. Destiny decrees that I shall be answered and the answer comes to me. Moreover, in other matters we never regulate our actions by the unknown decrees of God, as, for instance, a man never questions whether he shall eat or drink because it may or may not be decreed that he shall eat or drink—a man never inquires whether he shall work or not on the ground that it is decreed how much he shall do or how little. As it is inconsistent with common sense to make the secret decrees of God a guide to us in our general conduct, so we feel it should be in reference to prayer and therefore we still pray.

But we have a better answer than all this. Our Lord Jesus Christ comes forward and He says to us this morning, "My dear Children, the decrees of God need not trouble you. There is nothing in them inconsistent with your prayers being heard. 'I say unto you, ask, and it shall be given you.'" Now, who is He that says this? Why it is He that has been with the Father from the beginning—"the same was in the beginning with God"—and He knows what the purposes of the Father are and what the heart of God is, for He has told us in another place, "the Father Himself loves you." Now, since He knows the decrees of the Father and the heart of the Father, He can tell us with the absolute certainty of an eyewitness that there is nothing in the eternal purposes in conflict with this Truth of

God, that he that asks, receives, and he that seeks finds. He has read the decrees from beginning to end—has He not taken the Book and loosed the seven seals thereof and declared the ordinances of Heaven?

He tells you there is nothing there inconsistent with your bended knee and streaming eyes and with the Father's opening the windows of Heaven to shower upon you the blessings which you seek. Moreover, He is Himself God—the purposes of Heaven are His own purposes and He who ordained the purpose here gives the assurance that there is nothing in it to prevent the efficacy of prayer. "I say unto you." O you that believe in Him, your doubts are scattered to the winds—you know that He hears prayer!

But sometimes there arises in our mind a third difficulty which is associated with our own judgment of ourselves and our estimate of God. We feel that God is very great and we tremble in the presence of His majesty. We feel that we are very little and that, in addition, we are also vile—and it seems an incredible thing that such guilty nothings should have power to move the arm which moves the world! I wonder not if that fear should often hamper us in prayer. But Jesus answers it so sweetly. He says—"I say unto you, ask, and it shall be given you." And I ask again, who is it that says, "I say unto you"? Why, it is He who knows both the greatness of God and the weakness of man! He is God and out of the excellent Majesty I think I hear Him say, "I say unto you, ask, and it shall be given you."

But He is also Man, like ourselves, and He says, "Dread not your littleness, for I, bone of your bone and flesh of your flesh, assure you that God hears man's prayer." The words come to us with the harmony of blended notes! The God, the Man, both speak to us—"Dread not My majesty, your prayer is heard. Fear not your own weakness. I as a Man have been heard of God." And yet, again, if the dread of sin should haunt us and our own sorrow should depress us, I would remind you that Jesus Christ, when He says, "I say unto you," gives us the authority, not only of His person, but of His experience. Jesus was known to pray. Never any prayed as He did! Nights were spent in prayer by Him, and whole days in earnest intercession—and He says to us, "I say unto you, ask, and it shall be given you."

I think I see Him coming fresh from the heather of the hills, among which He had knelt all night to pray, and He says, "My disciples, ask, and it shall be given you, for I

have prayed and it has been given unto Me." I think I hear
Him say it with His face all bloody red and His garments
as if He had trod the wine vat, as He rises from Gethsemane with His soul exceedingly sorrowful even unto
death. He was heard in that He feared and therefore He
says to us, "I say unto you, knock and it shall be opened
unto you." Yes, and I think I hear Him speak thus from the
Cross, with His face bright with the first beam of sunlight
after He had borne our sins in His own body on the tree—
and had suffered all our griefs to the last pang. He had
cried, "My God, My God, why have You forsaken Me,"
and now, having received an answer, He cries in triumph,
"It is finished," and in so doing, bids us, also, "ask, and it
shall be given you." Jesus has proven the power of prayer!

"Oh but," says one, "He has not proven what it is to
pray in trouble like mine." How grossly you attest the Savior's trouble was worse than yours! There are no depths so
deep that He has not dived to the bottom of them! Christ
has prayed out of the lowest dungeon and out of the most
horrible pit. "Yes, but He has not cried under the burden of sin." How can you speak so thoughtlessly!? "Was
ever such a burden of sin borne by any man as was laid
on Him?" True, the sins were not His own, but they were
sins and sins with all their crushing weight in them, too!
Yet was He heard and He was helped unto the end. Christ
gives you, in His own experience, the divine proof that the
asking shall be followed by the receiving, even when sin
lies at the door.

Thus much is certain, if you, who are believers, cannot believe in the efficacy of prayer on the very Word of
Christ, it has come to a strange pass, for, O beloved, you
are leaning all your soul's weight on Jesus! If He is not
true, then you are trusting a false Savior! If He speaks not
truths of God, then you are deceived! If you can trust Him
with your soul, you must of necessity trust Him with your
prayers! Remember, too, that if Jesus our Lord could speak
so positively here, there is a yet greater reason for believing Him now, for He has gone within the veil—He sits
at the right hand of God, even the Father, and the voice
does not come to us from the Man of poverty, wearing a
garment without seam, but from the enthroned Priest with
the golden girdle about His loins, for it is He who now
says, from the right hand of God—"I say unto you, ask,
and it shall be given you."

Do you believe in His name? How, then, can a prayer

that is sincerely offered in that name fall to the ground?
When you present your petition in Jesus' name, a part of
His authority clothes your prayers. If your prayers are rejected, Christ is dishonored—surely, you cannot believe
that? You have trusted Him, then believe that prayer offered through Him must and shall win the day. We cannot
talk longer on this point, but we trust the Holy Spirit will
impress it upon all our hearts.

II. We will now remember that our Lord presents us
with a promise. Note that the promise is given to several
varieties of prayer. "I say unto you, ask, and it shall be
given you; seek, and you shall find; knock and it shall be
opened unto you." The text clearly asserts that all forms
of true prayer shall be heard, provided they are presented
through Jesus Christ and are for promised blessings. Some
are vocal prayers men ask—never should we fail to offer
up every day and continually the prayer which is uttered
by the tongue, for the promise is that the asker shall be
heard.

But there are others who, not neglecting vocal prayer,
are far more abundant in active prayer, for by humble and
diligent use of the means they seek the blessings which
they need. Their heart speaks to God by its longings, striv-
ings, emotions and labors. Let them not cease seeking, for
they shall surely find. There are others who, in their earnestness, combine the most eager forms, both acting and
speaking, for knocking is a loud kind of asking and a vehement form of seeking. If our prayers are vocal speech with
God, or if they are the practical use of means ordained,
which is real prayer—or if they should, best of all, be the
continued use of both—or if they are expressed only by a
tear or a sigh, or even if they remain quite unexpressed in
a trembling desire, they shall be heard. All varieties of true
prayer shall meet with responses from Heaven.

Now observe that these varieties of prayer are put on
an ascending scale. It is said first that we ask—I suppose
that refers to the prayer which is a mere statement of our
needs in which we tell the Lord that we need this and that
and ask Him to grant it to us. But as we learn the art of
prayer we go on further to seek—which signifies that we
marshal our arguments and plead reasons for the granting
of our desires—and we begin to wrestle with God for the
mercies needed. And if the blessings come not, we then
rise to the third degree which is knocking—we become
importunate—we are not content with asking and giving

reasons, but we throw the whole earnestness of our being into our requests and practice the text which says, "the kingdom of Heaven suffers violence and the violent take it by force."

So the prayers grow from asking—which is the statement, to seeking—which is the pleading, and to knocking—which is the importuning. To each of these stages of prayer there is a distinct promise. He that asks shall have—what did he ask for? But he that seeks, going further, shall find, shall enjoy, shall grasp, shall know that he has obtained. And he who knocks shall go further still, for he shall understand—and to him shall the precious thing be opened—he shall not merely have the blessing and enjoy it, but he will comprehend it! He shall "understand with all saints, what are the heights and depths."

I want, however, you to notice this fact, which covers all—whatever form your prayer may assume it shall succeed. If you only ask you shall receive. If you seek you shall find. If you knock it shall be opened. In each case, according to your faith, shall it be unto you. The clauses of the promise before us are not put, as we say, in law, jointly—he that asks and seeks and knocks shall receive—but they are put severally—he that asks shall have, he that seeks shall find, he that knocks shall have it opened. It is not when we combine the whole three that we get the blessing, though doubtless if we did combine them we should got the combined reply. But if we exercise only one of these three forms of prayer, we shall still get that which our souls seek after.

These three methods of prayer exercise a variety of our graces. It is a gloss of the fathers upon this passage that faith asks, hope seeks and love knocks—and the gloss is worth repeating. Faith asks because she believes God will give. Hope, having asked, expects, and therefore seeks for the blessing. Love comes nearer, still, and will not take a denial from God, but desires to enter into His house and to sup with Him and, therefore, knocks at His door till He opens. But, again, let us come back to the old point—it matters not which grace is exercised—a blessing comes to each one. If faith asks it shall receive. If hope seeks it shall find. And if love knocks it shall be opened to her.

These three modes of prayer suit us in different stages of distress. There am I, a poor mendicant at mercy's door. I ask and I shall receive—but I lose my way so that I cannot find Him of whom I once asked so successfully. Well, then,

I may seek with the certainty that I shall find. I am told if I am in the last stage of all, not merely poor and bewildered, but so defiled as to feel shut out from God like a leper shut out of the camp, then I may knock and the door will open to me. Each of these different descriptions of prayer is exceedingly simple. If anybody said, "I cannot ask," our reply would be, you do not understand the word. Surely everybody can ask! A little child can ask. Long before an infant can speak it can ask—it need not use words in order to ask for what it wants—and there is not one among us who is incapacitated from asking.

Prayers need not be fine. I believe God abhors fine prayers. If a person asks charity of you in elegant sentences he is not likely to get it. Finery in dress or language is out of place in boggles.[3] I heard a man in the street, one day, begging aloud by means of a magnificent oration. He used grand language in very pompous style and I dare say he thought he was sure of getting piles of coppers by his borrowed speech. But I, for one, gave him nothing. I felt more inclined to laugh at his bombast. Is it not likely that many great prayers are about as useless? Many prayer meetings' prayers are a great deal too fine. Keep your figures and metaphors and parabolic expressions for your fellow creatures! Use them for those who want to be instructed, but do not parade them before God! When we pray, the simpler our prayers are the better—the most plain, most humble language which expresses our meaning is the best.

The next word is 'seek' and surely there is no difficulty about seeking? In finding there might be, but in seeking there is none. When the woman in the parable lost her money she lit a candle and sought for it. I do not suppose she had ever been to the university, or qualified as a lady physician, or that she could have sat on the school board as a woman of superior sense—but she could seek. Anybody who desires to do so can seek—be they man, woman, or child—and for their encouragement the promise is not given to some particular philosophical form of seeking, but simply, "he that seeks finds."

Then there is knocking—well, that is a thing of no great difficulty. We used to do it when we were boys—sometimes too much for the neighbors' comfort! And at home, if the knocker was a little too high, we had ways and means of knocking at the door even then—a stone would do it, or the heel of a boot—anything would make a knock-

---

3   Beggars.

ing! It was not beyond our capacity by any means! Therefore, it is put in this fashion by Christ Himself, as much as
to tell us, "You need have no scholarship, no training, no
talent and no wit for prayer—ask, seek, knock—that is all,
and the promise is to everyone of these ways of praying."
Will you believe the promise? It is Christ who gives it! No
lie ever fell from His lips. O doubt Him not! Pray on if you
have prayed, but if you have never prayed before, God
help you to begin today!

III. Our third point is that Jesus testifies to the fact that
prayer is heard. Having given a promise He then adds,
in effect—"You may be quite sure that this promise will
be fulfilled, not only because I say it, but because it is and
always has been so." When a man says the sun will rise
tomorrow morning, we believe it because it has always ris-
en. Our Lord tells us that, as a matter of indisputable fact,
all along the ages true asking has been followed by receiving! Remember that He who stated this fact knew it. If you
state a fact you may reply, "Yes, as far as your observation goes, it is true." But the observation of Christ was un-
bounded. There was never a true prayer offered unknown
to Him! Prayers acceptable with the Most High come up
to Him by the way of the wounds of Christ. Therefore the
Lord Jesus Christ can speak by personal knowledge and
His declaration is that prayer has succeeded—"Everyone
that asks receives and he that seeks finds."

Now here we must, of course, suppose the limitations
which would be made by ordinary common sense and
which are made by Scripture. It is not everyone that frivo-
lously or wickedly asks or pretends to ask of God that gets
what he asks for. It is not every silly, idle, unconsidered
request of unregenerate hearts that God will answer. By
no manner of means—common sense limits the statement
so far. Besides, Scripture limits it again, "You have not because you ask not, or because you ask amiss"—there is an
asking amiss which will never obtain. If we ask that we
may consume the good things upon our lust we shall not
have them. If we ask for that which would not be to our
good we shall be heard by receiving no such answer as
we desired. But those things being remembered, the statement of our Lord has no other qualification—"everyone
that asks receives."

Let it be remembered that frequently, even when the
ungodly and the wicked have asked of God, they have received. Full often in the time of their distress they have

called upon God and He has answered them. "How can you say that" asks one. No, I say not so, but so says Scripture. Ahab's prayer was answered and the Lord said, "see you how Ahab humbles himself before Me? Because he humbles himself before Me, I will not bring the evil in his days: but in his son's days will I bring the evil upon his house." So, also, the Lord heard the prayer of Jehoahaz, the son of Jehu, who did evil in the sight of the Lord. (2 Kings 13:1-4). The Israelites, also, when for their sins were given over to their foes, cried to God for deliverance and they were answered—yet the Lord Himself testified concerning them that they did but flatter with their mouth.

Does this stagger you? Does He not hear the young ravens when they cry? Do you think He will not hear man, that is formed in His own image? Do you doubt it? Remember Nineveh! The prayers offered at Nineveh—were they spiritual prayers? Did you ever hear of a church of God in Nineveh? I have not, neither do I believe the Ninevites were ever visited by converting grace—but they were, by the preaching of Jonah, convicted that they were in danger from the great Jehovah—and they proclaimed a fast and humbled themselves! And God heard their prayer and Nineveh, for a while, was preserved. Many a time in the hour of sickness and in the time of woe, God has heard the prayers of the unthankful and the evil. Do you think God gives nothing except to the good? Have you dwelt at the foot of Sinai and learned to judge according to the Law of merit? What were you when you did begin to pray? Were you good and righteous? Has not God commanded you to do good to the evil? Will He command you to do what He will not do Himself?

Has He not said that He "sends rain upon the just and upon the unjust" and is it not so? Is He not daily blessing those who curse Him and doing good to those who despitefully use Him? This is one of the glories of God's Grace and when there is nothing else good in the man, yet if there is a cry lifted up from his heart, the Lord deigns full often to send relief from trouble. Now, if God has heard the prayers even of men who have not sought Him in the highest manner and has given them temporary deliverances in answer to their cries, will He not much more hear you when you are humbling yourself in His sight and desiring to be reconciled to Him? Surely there is an argument here!

But to come more fully to the point with regard to

real and spiritual prayers, everyone that asks receives without any limit whatever. There has never been an instance, yet, of a man really seeking spiritual blessings of God without his receiving them. The publican stood afar off and so broken was his heart that he dared not look up to Heaven—yet God looked down on him. Manasseh lay in the low dungeon. He had been a cruel persecutor of the saints. There was nothing in him that could commend him to God, but God heard him out of the dungeon and brought him forth to liberty of soul. Jonah had, by his own sin, brought himself into the whale's belly and he was a petulant servant of God at the best—but out of the belly of Hell he cried and God heard him. "Everyone that asks receives and he that seeks finds; and to him that knocks it shall be opened." Everyone!

If I needed evidence I should be able to find it in this Tabernacle. I would ask anyone here who has found Christ to bear witness that God heard his prayer. I do not believe that among the damned in Hell there is one who dares say, "I sought the Lord and He rejected me." There shall not be found, at the last day of account, one single soul that can say, "I knocked at Mercy's door, but God refused to open it." There shall not stand before the Great White Throne a single soul that can plead, "O Christ, I would have been saved by You, but You would not save me! I gave myself up into Your hands, but You did reject me. I penitently asked for mercy of You, but I had it not." Everyone that asks receives. It has been so until this day—it will be so till Christ Himself shall come. If you doubt it try it and if you have tried it try it again.

Are you in rags?—that matters not—everyone that asks receives. Are you foul with sin?—that matters not—"everyone that seeks finds." Do you feel yourself as if you were shut out from God altogether?—that matters not, either—"knock, and it shall be opened unto you, for everyone that asks receives." "Is there no election there?" Yes, yes, doubtless there is! But that does not alter this truth of God which has no limit to it whatever—"everyone." What a rich text it is! "Everyone that asks receives." When our Lord spoke thus, He could have pointed to His own life as evidence—at any rate we can refer to it now and show that no one asked of Christ who did not receive. The Syro-Phoenician woman was at first repulsed when the Lord called her a dog. But when she had the courage to say, "Yet the dogs eat the crumbs that fall from the table," she soon discovered that everyone that asks receives.

She, also, who came behind Him in the crowd and touched the hem of His garment—she was no asker, but she was a seeker—and she found. I think I hear, in answer to all this, the lamentable wail of one who says, "I have been crying to God a long while for salvation. I have asked, I have sought and I have knocked, but it has not come yet." Well, dear friend, if I am asked which is true, God or you, I know which I shall stand by and I would advise you to believe God before you believe yourself! God will hear prayer, but do you know there is one thing before prayer? What is it? Why, the Gospel is not—"he that prays shall be saved"—that is not the Gospel! I believe he will be saved, but that is not the Gospel. I am told to preach to you. "Go you into all the world and preach the Gospel to every creature; he"—what?—"he that believes and is baptized shall be saved."

Now, you have been asking God to save you—do you expect Him to save you without your believing and being baptized? Surely you have not had the impudence to ask God to make void His own Word! Might He not say to you, "Do as I bid you. Believe My Son. He that believes on Him has everlasting life." Let me ask you, do you believe Jesus Christ? Will you trust Him? "Oh, I trust Him," says one. "I trust Him wholly." Soul, do not ask for salvation any more—you have it already—you are saved! If you trust Jesus with all your soul, your sins are forgiven you and you are saved. And the next time you approach the Lord, go with praise as well as with prayer and sing and bless His name.

"But how am I to know that I am saved?" asks one. God says, "He that believes and is baptized shall be saved." Have you believed? Have you been baptized? If so, you are saved. How do I know that? On the best evidence in all the world—God says you are—do you need any evidence but that? "I want to feel this." Feel! Are your feelings better than God's witness? Will you make God a liar by asking more signs and tokens than His sure Word of Testimony? I have no evidence this day that I dare trust in concerning my salvation but this—that I rest on Christ alone with all my heart, soul and strength. "Other refuge have I none," and if you have that evidence, it is all the evidence that you need seek for this day. Other witnesses of divine grace in your heart shall come, by-and-by, and cluster about you and adorn the doctrines you do profess—but now your first business is to believe in Jesus.

"I have asked for faith," says one. Well, what do you mean by that? To believe in Jesus Christ is the gift of God, but it must be your own act as well. Do you think God will believe for you, or that the Holy Spirit believes instead of us? What has the Holy Spirit to believe? You must believe for yourself or be lost! He cannot lie—will you not believe in Him? He deserves to be believed! Trust in Him and you are saved, and your prayer is answered! I think I hear another say, "I trust I am already saved, but I have been looking for the salvation of others in answer to my prayers." Dear friend, you will get it. "He that asks receives and he that seeks finds; and to him that knocks it shall be opened." "But I have sought the conversion of such an one for years with many prayers."

You shall have it, or you shall know one day why you have it not and shall be made content not to have it! Pray on in hope. Many a one has had his prayer for others answered after he has been dead. I think I have reminded you before of the father who had prayed for many years for his sons and daughters and yet they were not convert-ed. In fact, all of them became exceedingly worldly. His time came to die. He gathered his children about his bed, hoping to bear such a witness for Christ at the last that it might be blessed to their conversion—but unhappily for him he was in deep distress of soul. He had doubts about his own interest in Christ. He was one of God's children who are put to bed in the dark—this being, above all, the worst fear of his mind, that he feared his dear children would see his distress and be prejudiced against religion.

The good man was buried and his sons came to the funeral—and God heard the man's prayer that very day—for as they went away from the grave one of them said to the other, "Brother, our father died a most unhappy death." "He did, brother. I was very much astonished at it, for I never knew a better man than our father." "Ah," said the first brother, "if a holy man such as our father found it a hard thing to die, it will be a dreadful thing for us who have no faith when our time comes." That same thought had struck them all and drove them to the cross—and so the good man's prayer was heard in a mysterious manner.

Heaven and earth shall pass away, but while God lives, prayer must be heard. While God remains true to His Word, supplication is not in vain! The Lord give you divine grace to exercise it continually. Amen.

II. The Ravens' Cry

He gives to the beast his food, and to the young
ravens which cry.
Psalm 147:9.

I shall open this sermon with a quotation. I must give you, in Caryl's own words his note upon ravens. "Naturalists tell us that when the raven hath fed his young in the nest till they are well fledged and able to fly abroad, he thrusts them out of the nest and will not let them abide there, but puts them out to get their own living. Now when these young ones are upon their first flight from their nest and are little acquainted with means how to help themselves with food, then the Lord provides food for them. It is said by credible authorities that the raven is marvelously strict and severe in this—as soon as his young ones are able to provide for themselves, he will not fetch any more food for them. Some affirm the old ones will not suffer them to stay in the same country where they were bred, and if so, then they must wander. We say proverbially, 'Need makes the old wife trot;' we may say, 'and the young ones too.' It has been, and possibly is, the practice of some parents towards their children, who, as soon as they can shift for themselves and are fit in any competency to get their bread, to turn them out of doors as the raven does his young ones out of the nest. Now, said the Lord in the text, when the young ones of the raven are in this pinch, that they are turned off, and wander for lack of meat, who, then, provides for them? Do not I, the Lord? Do not I, who provide for the old raven, provide for his young ones, both while they abide in the nest and when they wander for lack of meat?"

Solomon sent the sluggard to the ant, and learned himself, lessons from conies, greyhounds, and spiders! Let us be willing to be instructed by any of God's creatures and go to the ravens' nest tonight to learn as in a school. To the pure nothing is unclean, and to the wise nothing is trivial. Let the superstitious dread the raven as a bird of ill omen, and let the thoughtless see nothing but a winged thing in glossy black—we are willing to see more, and doubtless shall not be unrewarded if we are but teachable.

Noah's raven brought him back no olive branch, but ours may! And it may even come to pass that ravens may bring us meat tonight as of old they fed Elijah by Cherith's brook. Our blessed Lord once derived a very potent argument from ravens—an argument intended to comfort and cheer those of His servants who were oppressed with needless anxieties about their temporal circumstances. To such he said, "Consider the ravens: for they neither sow nor reap, which neither have storehouse nor barn, and God feeds them. How much more are you better than the fowls?"

Following the Master's logic—which you will all agree must have been sound, for He was never untruthful in His reasoning any more than in His statements—I shall argue tonight on this wise: Consider the ravens as they cry! With harsh, inarticulate, croaking notes they make known their needs, and your heavenly Father answers their prayer and sends them food! You, too, have begun to pray and to seek His favor—are you not much better than they? Does God care for ravens, and will he not care for you? Does He not hearken to the cries of the unfledged ravens in their nests when they are hungry and cry unto Him to be fed?

Does He, I say, supply them in answer to their cries, and will He not answer you, poor trembling children of men who are seeking His face and favor through Christ Jesus? The whole business of this evening will be just simply to work that one thought out. I shall aim tonight, under the guidance of the Holy Spirit, to say something to those who have been praying for mercy but as yet have not received it—who have gone on their knees, perhaps, for months, with one exceeding great and bitter cry—but as yet know not the way of peace.

Their sin still hangs like a millstone about their neck. They sit in the valley of the shadow of death. No light has dawned upon them and they are wringing their hands and moaning, "Has God forgotten to be gracious? Has He shut His ear against the prayers of seeking souls? Will He be mindful of sinners' piteous cries no more? Will penitents' tears drop upon the earth and no longer move His compassion?" Satan, too, is telling you, dear friends, who are now in this state of mind, that God will never hear you. That He will let you cry till you die! That you shall pant out your life in sighs and tears and that at the end you shall be cast into the Lake of Fire!

I long, tonight, to give you some comfort and encouragement. I want to urge you to cry yet more vehemently! Come to the cross and lay hold of it, and vow that you will never leave its shadow till you find the gift which your soul covets. I want to move you, if God the Holy Spirit shall help me, so that you will say within yourselves, like Queen Esther, "I will go in unto the King, and if I perish, I perish." And may you add to that the vow of Jacob, "I will not let You go, except You bless me!" Here, then, is the question in hand: God hears the young ravens. will he not hear you?

I. I argue that He will, first, when I remember that He hears the lowly raven cry, and that you, in some sense, are much better than a raven. The raven is but a poor unclean bird whose instant death would make no sort of grievous gap in creation. If thousands of ravens had their necks wrung tomorrow I do not know that there would be any vehement grief and sorrow in the universe about them! It would simply be a number of poor birds dead, and that would be all.

But you are an immortal soul! The raven is gone when life is over—there is no raven any longer. But when your present life is past, you have not ceased to be—you are but launched upon the sea of life—you have but begun to live forever. You will see earth's hoary mountains crumble to nothingness before your immortal spirit shall expire! The moon shall have paled her feeble light, and the sun's more mighty fires shall have been quenched in perpetual darkness, and yet your spirit shall still be marching on in its everlasting course—an everlasting course of misery, unless God hears your cry—

"Oh, that truth immense,
    This mortal, immortality shall wear!
    The pulse of mind shall never cease to play;
    By God awakened, it forever throbs,
    Eternal as His own eternity!
    Above the angels, or below the fiends:
    To mount in Glory, or in shame descend—
    Mankind is destined by resistless doom."

Do you think, then, that God will hear the poor bird that is and is not—is here a moment and is blotted out of existence—and will He not hear you, an immortal soul, whose duration is to be co-equal with His own? I think it surely must strike you that if He hears the dying raven He will also hear an undying man. The ancients said of Jupiter that he was not at leisure to mind little things, but Jehovah condescends to care for the least of His creatures, and even looks into birds' nests! Will He not mercifully care for spirits who are heirs of a dread eternity?

Moreover, I never heard that ravens were made in the image of God! But I do find that, defiled, deformed, and debased as our race is, yet originally God said, "Let Us make man in Our own image." There is something about man which is not to be found in the lower creatures, the best and noblest of whom are immeasurably beneath the meanest child of Adam. A council was held as to the creation of man, and in his mind, and even in the adaptation of his body to assist the mind, there is a marvelous display of the wisdom of the Most High.

Bring here the most deformed, obscure and wicked of the human race, and—though I dare not flatter human nature morally—yet there is a dignity about the fact of manhood which is not to be found in all the beasts of the field, be they what they may. Behemoth and Leviathan are put in subjection beneath the foot of man. The eagle cannot soar so high as man's soul mounts, nor the lion feed on such royal meat as man's spirit hungers after. And do you think that God will hear so low and so mean a creature as a raven and yet not hear you, when you are one of the race that was formed in His own image?

Oh, think not so harshly and so foolishly of Him whose ways are always equal! I will put this to yourselves. Does not nature itself teach that man is to be cared for above the fowls of the air? If you heard the cries of young ravens, you might feel compassion enough for those birds to give them food if you knew how to feed them. But I cannot believe that any of you would succor the birds, and yet would not fly upon the wings of compassion to the rescue of a perishing infant whose cries you might hear from the place where it was cast by cruel neglect! If, in the stillness of the night, you heard the plaintive cry of a man expiring in sickness, unpitied in the streets, would you not arise and help him?

I am sure you would if you are one who would help a raven. If you have any compassion for a raven, surely much more would you have pity upon a man! I know it is whispered that there are some simpletons who care more

for houseless dogs than for houseless men and women—
and yet it is far more probable that those who feel for dogs
are those who care most tenderly for men. At any rate, I
should feel a strong presumption in their favor if I needed aid. And do you not think that God, the All-Wise One,
when He cares for these unfledged birds in the nest, will
be sure also to care for you?

Your heart says, "Yes." Then from now on answer the
unbelief of your heart by turning its own just reasoning
against it. But I hear you say, "Ah, but the raven is not
sinful as I am! It may be an unclean bird, but it cannot be
so unclean as I am morally. It may be black in hue, but I
am black with sin! A raven cannot break the Sabbath, cannot swear, cannot commit adultery! A raven cannot be a
drunkard! It cannot defile itself with vices such as those
with which I am polluted."

I know all that, friend, and it may seem to you to
make your case more hopeless, but I do not think it really does so. Just think of it for a minute. What does this
prove? Why, that you are a creature capable of sinning,
and, consequently, that you are an intelligent spirit living
in a sense in which a raven does not live. You are a creature
moving in the spirit-world! You belong to the world of
souls in which the raven has no portion. The raven cannot
sin, because it has no spirit, no soul. But you are an intelligent agent of which the better part is your soul. Now, as
the soul is infinitely more precious than the body! And as
the raven—I am speaking popularly now—is nothing but
body while you are evidently soul as well as body—or else
you would not be capable of sinning—I see even in that
black discouraging thought some gleam of light!

Does God care for flesh, and blood, and bones, and
black feathers, and will He not care for your reason, your
will, your judgment, your conscience, your immortal soul?
Oh, if you will but think of it, you must see that it is not
possible for a raven's cry to gain an audience of the ear
of Divine Benevolence and for your prayer to be despised
and disregarded by the Most High—

> "The insect that with puny wings,
> Just shoots along one summer's ray.
> The flower which the breath of Spring
> Wakes into life for half a day.
> The smallest mote, the most tender hair,
> All feel our heavenly Father's care."

Surely, then, He will have respect unto the cry of the humble, and will not refuse their prayer!

I can hardly leave this point without remarking that the mention of a raven should encourage a sinner. As an old author writes, "Among fowls He does not mention the hawk or falcon, which are highly prized and fed by princes. But He chooses that hateful and malicious bird, the croaking raven, whom no man values but as she eats up the carrion which might annoy him. Behold then, and wonder at the providence and kindness of God, that He should provide food for the raven, a creature of so dismal a hue and of so untuneable a tone—a creature that is so odious to most men, and ominous to some. There is a great providence of God seen in providing for the ant, who gathers her meat in summer—but a greater in the raven, who, though he forgets, or is careless to provide for himself, yet God provides and lays up for him."

One would think the Lord should say of ravens, let them shift for themselves or perish! No, the Lord God does not despise any work of His hands. The raven has his being from God, and therefore the raven shall be provided for by Him. Not only the fair innocent dove, but the ugly raven has his meat from God. Which clearly shows that the want of excellence in you, you black, raven-like sinner, will not prevent your cry from being heard in Heaven! Unworthiness the blood of Jesus shall remove, and defilement He shall utterly cleanse away. Only believe on Jesus, and you shall find peace!

II. Then, in the next place, there is a great deal of difference between your cry and the cry of a raven. When the young ravens cry I suppose they scarcely know what they want. They have a natural instinct which makes them cry for food, but their cry does not, in itself, express their need. You would soon find out, I suppose, that they meant food—but they have no articulate speech—they do not utter so much as a single word! It is just a constant, croaking, craving cry and that is all.

But you know what you need, and few as your words are, your heart knows its own bitterness and dire distress. Your sighs and groans have an obvious meaning. Your understanding is at the right hand of your hungry heart. You know that you want peace and pardon. You know that you need Jesus, His precious blood, His perfect righteousness.

Now, if God hears such a strange, chattering, indistinct cry as that of a raven, don't you think that He will also hear the rational and expressive prayer of a poor, needy, guilty soul who is crying unto Him, "God be merciful to me a sinner"? Surely your reason tells you that!

Moreover, the young ravens cannot use arguments, for they have no understanding. They cannot say as you can—

"He knows what arguments I'd take
To wrestle with my God,
I'd plead for His own mercy's sake,
And for a Savior's blood."

They have one argument, namely, their dire necessity, which forces their cry from them, but beyond this they cannot go. And even this they cannot set forth in order, or describe in language. But you have a multitude of arguments ready at hand, and you have an understanding with which to set them in array and marshal them to besiege the Throne of Grace. Surely, if the mere plea of the unuttered need of the raven prevails with God, much more shall you prevail with the Most High if you can argue your case before Him and come unto Him with arguments in your mouth! Come, despairing one, and try my Lord! I do beseech you, now, let that doleful ditty ascend into the ears of mercy! Open that bursting heart and let it out in tears if words are beyond your power!

A raven, however, I fear has sometimes a great advantage over some sinners who seek God in prayer, namely in this: young ravens are more in earnest about their food than some are about their souls. This, however, is no discouragement to you, but rather a reason why you should be more earnest than you have been. When ravens need food, they do not cease crying till they have it. There is no quieting a hungry young raven till his mouth is full, and there is no quieting a sinner when he is really in earnest till he gets his heart full of divine mercy. I would that some of you prayed more vehemently! "The kingdom of Heaven suffers violence, and the violent take it by force."

An old Puritan said, "Prayer is a cannon set at the gate of Heaven to burst open its gates." You must take the city by storm if you would have it! You will not ride to Heaven on a featherbed. You must go on pilgrimage—there is no going to the land of Glory while you are sound asleep—dreamy sluggards will have to wake up in Hell! If God has made you to feel in your soul the need of salvation, cry like one who is awake and alive! Be in earnest! Cry aloud!

Spare not! And then I think you will find that my argument will be quite fair—that in all respects a reasonable,
argumentative, intelligent prayer is more likely to prevail
with God than the mere screaming, chattering noise of the
raven—and that if He hears such a cry as the raven's—it is
much more certain that He will hear yours.

III. Remember that the matter of your prayer is more
congenial to the ear of God than the raven's cry for meat.
All that the young ravens call for is food—give them a little carrion[4] and they have done. Your cry must be much
more pleasing to God's ear, for you entreat for forgiveness
through the blood of His dear Son. It is a nobler occupa-
tion for the Most High to be bestowing spiritual than natural gifts. The streams of divine grace flow from the up-
per springs. I know He is so condescending that He does
not dishonor Himself even when He drops food into the
young raven's mouth, but still there is more honor about
the work of giving peace, and pardon, and reconciliation
to the sons of men.

Eternal love appointed a way of mercy from before the
foundation of the world, and infinite wisdom is engaged
with boundless power to carry out the divine design. Surely the Lord must take much pleasure in saving the sons of
men! If God is pleased to supply the beast of the field, do
you not think that He delights much more to supply His
own children? I think you would find more congenial em-
ployment in teaching your own children than you would
in merely foddering your ox, or scattering barley among
the fowls at the barn door because there would be in the
first work something nobler, which would more fully call
up all your powers and bring out your inward self.

I am not left here to conjecture. It is written, "He delights in mercy." When God uses His power He cannot
be sad, for He is a happy God. But if there is such a thing
possible as the infinite deity being more happy at one
time than at another, it is when He is forgiving sinners
through the precious blood of Jesus. Ah, sinner, when you
cry to God you give Him an opportunity to do that which
He loves most to do! He delights to forgive, to press His
Ephraim to His bosom, to say of His prodigal son, "He was
lost, but is found. He was dead, but is alive again." This is
more comfortable to the Father's heart than the feeding of
the fatted calf, or tending the cattle of a thousand hills.

Since then, dear friends, you are asking for something

---

4   The decaying flesh of dead animals.

which will honor God far more to give than the mere gift
of food to ravens, I think there comes a very forcible blow
of my argumentative hammer tonight to break your unbelief in pieces! May God the Holy Spirit, the true comforter,
work in you mightily! Surely the God who gives food to
ravens will not deny peace and pardon to seeking sinners.
Try Him! Try Him at this moment! No, stir not! Try Him
now!

IV. We must not pause on any one point when the
whole subject is so prolific. There is another source of
comfort for you, namely, that the ravens are nowhere commanded to cry. When they cry, their petition is unwarrant-
ed by any specific exhortation from the divine mouth. But
you have a warrant derived from divine exhortations to
approach the Throne of God in prayer!

If a rich man should open his house to those who were
not invited he would surely receive those who were invited. Ravens come without being bid to come, yet they
are not sent away empty! You are commanded to come as
an invited guest—how shall you be denied? Do you think
you are not bid to come? Listen to this: "Whoever calls on
the name of the Lord shall be saved." "Call upon Me in the
day of trouble, and I will deliver you, and you shall glorify
Me." "Go you into all the world, and preach the Gospel
to every creature. He that believes and is baptized shall
be saved. He that believes not shall be damned." "Believe
in the Lord Jesus Christ and you shall be saved." "Repent
and be baptized, every one of you, in the name of the Lord
Jesus."

These are exhortations given without any limitation
as to character. They freely invite you—no, they bid you
come. Oh, after this can you think that God will spurn
you? The window is open, the raven flies in and the God
of mercy does not chase it out! The door is open, and the
word of promise bids you come—don't think that He will
deny you, but believe rather that He will "receive you graciously and love you freely," and then you shall "render
to Him the calves of your lips." At any rate try Him! Try
Him even now!

V. Again, there is yet another and a far mightier argument. The cry of a young raven is nothing but the natural
cry of a creature, but your cry, if it is sincere, is the result
of a work of divine grace in your heart. When the raven
cries to Heaven it is nothing but the raven's own self that
cries—but when you cry, "God be merciful to me a sin-

ner" — it is God the Holy Spirit crying in you!

It is the new life which God has given you crying to the source from where it came to have communion and communication with its great original. It needs God Himself to set a man praying in sincerity and in truth! We can, if we think about it, teach our children to "say their prayers," but we cannot teach them to "pray." You may make a "prayer-book," but you cannot put a grain of "prayer" into a book, for it is too spiritual a matter to be encased between leaves. Some of you, perhaps, may "read prayers" in the family. I will not denounce the practice but I will say this much of it — you may read those "prayers" for seventy years and yet you may never once pray — for prayer is quite a different thing from mere words.

True prayer is the trading of the heart with God, and the heart never comes into spiritual commerce with the ports of Heaven until God the Holy Spirit puts wind into the sails and speeds the ship into its haven. "You must be born again." If there is any real prayer in your heart, though you may not know the secret, God the Holy Spirit is there! Now if He hears cries that do not come from Himself, how much more will He hear those that do! Perhaps you have been puzzling yourself to know whether your cry is a natural or a spiritual one. This may seem very important, and doubtless is so — but whether your cry is either the one or the other, still continue to seek the Lord!

Possibly you doubt whether natural cries are heard by God. Let me assure you that they are. I remember saying something on this subject on one occasion in a certain ultra-Calvinistic place of worship. At that time I was preaching to children and was exhorting them to pray. I happened to say that long before any actual conversion I had prayed for common mercies, and that God had heard my prayers. This did not suit my good brethren of the superfine school! And afterwards they all came round me professedly to know what I meant, but really to cavil and carp according to their nature and practice.

"They compassed me about like bees. Yes, like bees they compassed me about!" After awhile, as I expected, they fell to their usual amusement of calling names. They began to say what rank Arminianism this was! And another expression they were pleased to honor me with, was the title of "Fullerist" — a title, by the way, so honorable that I could heartily have thanked them for appending it to what I had advanced! But to say that God should hear

the prayer of natural men was something worse than Arminianism to them, if, indeed, anything could be worse!
They quoted that counterfeit passage, "The prayer of the
wicked is an abomination unto the Lord," which I speedily
answered by asking them if they would find me that text
in the Word of God, for I ventured to assert that the devil
was the author of that saying, and that it was not in the
Bible at all.

"The sacrifice of the wicked is an abomination unto
the Lord" is in the Bible, but that is a very different thing
from the "prayer of the wicked." And moreover there is a
decided difference between the word wicked there intended and the natural man about whom we were arguing. I
do not think that a man who begins to pray in any sense
can be considered as being altogether among "the wicked"
intended by Solomon, and certainly he is not among those
who turn away their ears from hearing the Law, of whom
it is written that their prayer is an abomination.

"Well, but," they said, "how could it be that God could
hear a natural prayer?" And while I paused for a moment,
an old woman in a red cloak pushed her way into the little circle round me and said to them in very forcible way,
like a mother in Israel as she was, "Why do you raise this
question, forgetting what God Himself has said! What is
this you say, that God does not hear natural prayer? Why,
doesn't He hear the young ravens when they cry unto
Him? And do you think they offer spiritual prayers?"

Straightway the men of war took to their heels—no
defeat was more thorough—and for once in their lives they
must have felt that they might possibly err! Surely, brethren, this may encourage and comfort you! I am not going
to set you just now to the task of finding out whether your
prayers are natural or spiritual—whether they come from
God's Spirit or whether they do not—because that might,
perhaps, discourage you. If the prayer proceeds from your
very heart, we know how it got there, though you may
not. God hears the ravens, and I do believe He will hear
you, and I believe, moreover, though I do not now want to
raise the question in your heart, that He hears your prayer,
because—though you may not know it—there is a secret
work of the Spirit of God going on within you which is
teaching you to pray.

VI. But I have mightier arguments and nearer the
mark. When the young ravens cry, they cry alone. But
when you pray you have a mightier One than you praying

with you! Hear that sinner crying, "God be merciful to me a sinner"? Hark! Do you hear that other cry which goes up with his? No, you do not hear it because your ears are dull and heavy, but God hears it. There is another voice, far louder and sweeter than the first, and far more prevalent, mounting up at the same moment and pleading, "Father, forgive them through My precious blood."

The echo to the sinner's whisper is as majestic as the thunder's peal! Never sinner prays truly without Christ praying at the same time! You cannot see nor hear Him, but never does Jesus stir the depths of your soul by His Spirit without His soul being stirred, too. Oh, sinner, your prayer, when it comes before God, is a very different thing from what it is when it issues forth from you!

Sometimes poor people come to us with petitions which they wish to send to some company or great personage. They bring the petition and ask us to have it presented for them. It is very badly spelt, very strangely written, and we can but just make out what they mean. But still, there is enough to let us know what they need. First of all we make out a fair copy for them, and then, having stated their case, we put our own name at the bottom. And if we have any interest, of course they get what they desire through the power of the name signed at the foot of the petition.

This is just what the Lord Jesus Christ does with our poor prayers! He makes a fair copy of them, stamps them with the seal of His own atoning blood, puts His own name at the foot, and thus they go up to God's Throne. It is your prayer, but oh, it is His prayer, too! And it is the fact of its being His prayer that makes it prevail. Now, this is a sledge hammer argument—if the ravens prevail when they cry all alone, if their poor chattering brings them what they need of themselves—how much more shall the plaintive petitions of the poor trembling sinner prevail who can say, "For Jesus' sake," and who can clench all his own arguments with the blessed plea, "The Lord Jesus Christ deserves it! O Lord, give it to me for His sake"?

I do trust that these seeking ones to whom I have been speaking, who have been crying so long and yet are afraid that they shall never be heard, may not have to wait much longer but may soon have a gracious answer of peace! And if they shall not just yet get the desire of their hearts, I hope that they may be encouraged to persevere till the day of grace shall dawn. You have a promise which the ravens have not, and that might make another argument if time permitted us to dwell upon it. Trembler, having a promise to plead, never fear but that you shall be heard at the Throne of Grace!

And now, let me say to the sinner, in closing, if you have cried unsuccessfully, still cry on. "Go again seven times," yes, and seventy times seven! Remember that the mercy of God in Christ Jesus is your only hope!

Cling to it, then, as a drowning man clings to the only rope within reach. If you perish praying for mercy through the precious blood, you will be the first that ever perished so! Cry on! Just cry on! But oh, believe, too! For believing brings the morning star and the day dawn.

When John Ryland's wife, Betty, lay dying, she was in great distress of mind, though she had been for many years a Christian. Her husband said to her in his quaint but wise way, "Well, Betty, what ails you?" "Oh, John, I am dying, and I have no hope, John!" "But, my Dear, where are you going then?" "I am going to Hell!" was the answer. "Well," said he, covering up his deep anguish with his usual humor, and meaning to strike a blow that would be sure to hit the nail on the head and put her doubts to speedy flight, "What do you intend doing when you get there, Betty?" The good woman could give no answer, and Mr. Ryland continued, "Do you think you will pray when you get there?"

"Oh, John," said she, "I should pray anywhere. I cannot help praying!" "Well, then," said he, "they will say, 'Here is Betty Ryland praying here. Turn her out! We won't have anybody praying here! Turn her out!'" This strange way of putting it brought light to her soul and she saw at once the absurdity of the very suspicion of a soul really seeking Christ, and yet being cast away forever from His presence! Cry on, soul! Cry on! While the child can cry, it lives. And while you can besiege the Throne of Mercy, there is hope for you! But hear as well as cry, and believe what you hear, for it is by believing that peace is obtained.

But stay awhile, I have something else to say. Is it possible that you may have already obtained the very blessing you are crying after? "Oh," you say, "I would not ask for a thing which I had already got! If I knew I had it, I would leave off crying, and begin praising and blessing God." Now, I do not know whether all of you seekers are in so safe a state, but I am persuaded that there are some seeking souls who have received the mercy for which they are asking. The Lord, instead of saying to them tonight, "Seek you My face," is saying, "Why cry you unto Me? I have heard you in an acceptable hour, and in an acceptable time have I succored you. I have blotted out your sins like a cloud, and like a thick cloud your iniquities. I have saved you. You are Mine. I have cleansed you from all your sins. Go your way and rejoice."

In such a case believing praise is more suitable than agonizing prayer. "Oh," you say, "But it is not likely that I have the mercy while I am still seeking for it." Well, I do not know. Mercy sometimes falls down in a fainting fit outside the gate. Is it not possible for her to be taken inside while she is in the fainting fit, and for her to think all the while that she is still on the outside? She can hear the dog still barking, but ah, poor soul, when she comes to, she will find that she is inside the wicket and is safe!

So some of you may happen to have fallen into a swoon of despondency just when you are coming to Christ. If so, may sovereign grace restore you, and perhaps I may be the means, tonight, of doing it. What is it you are looking after? Some of you are expecting to see bright visions, but I hope you never may be gratified for they are not worth a penny a thousand. All the visions in the world since the days of miracles, put together, are but mere dreams, after all—and dreams are nothing but vanity! People eat too much supper and then dream—it is indigestion, or a morbid activity of the brain—and that is all! If that is all the evidence you have of conversion you will do well to doubt it. I pray you never to rest satisfied with it—it is wretched rubbish to build your eternal hopes upon.

Perhaps you are looking for very strange feelings—not quite an electric shock, but something very singular and peculiar. Believe me, you need never feel the strange motions which you prize so highly. All those strange feelings which some people speak of in connection with conversion may or may not be of any good to them, but I am certain that they really have nothing to do with conversion so as to be at all necessary to it!

I will put a question or two to you. Do you believe yourself to be a sinner? "Yes," you say. But supposing I put that word "sinner" away? Do you mean that you believe you have broken God's Law, that you are a good-for-nothing offender against God's government? Do you believe that you have in your heart, at any rate, broken all the Commandments, and that you deserve punishment

accordingly? "Yes," you say, "I not only believe that, but
I feel it! It is a burden that I carry about with me daily."

Now something more—do you believe that the Lord
Jesus Christ can put all this sin of yours away? Yes, you
do believe that. Then, can you trust Him to save you? You
need saving. You cannot save yourself. Can you trust Him
to save you? "Yes," you say, "I already do that." Well,
my dear friend, if you really trust Jesus, it is certain that
you are saved, for you have the only evidence of salvation which is continual with any of us! There are other evidences which follow afterwards, such as holiness and the
graces of the Spirit, but the only evidence that is continual
with the best of men living is this—

"Nothing in my hands I bring,
  Simply to Your Cross I cling."

Can you use Jack the huckster's verse—

"I'm a poor sinner and nothing at all,
  But Jesus Christ is my All in All"?

I hope you will go a great deal farther in experience on
some points than this, by and by, but I do not want you to
advance an inch farther as to the ground of your evidence
and the reason for your hope. Just stop there and if now
you look away from everything that is within you or without you to Jesus Christ, and trust to His sufferings on Calvary and to His whole atoning work as the ground of your
acceptance before God, you are saved! You do not need
anything more! You have passed from death unto life. "He
that believes on Him is not condemned." "He that believes
has everlasting life."

If I were to meet an angel presently in that aisle as I
go out of my door into my vestry, and he should say—
"Charles Spurgeon, I have come from Heaven to tell you
that you are pardoned," I should say to him—"I know that
without your telling me anything of the kind! I know it on
a great deal better authority than yours." And if he asked
me how I knew it, I should reply, "The Word of God is
better to me than the word of an angel, and He has said
it—'He that believes on Him is not condemned.' I do believe on Him, and therefore I am not condemned—and I
know it without an angel to tell me so."

Do not, you troubled ones, be looking after angels,
and tokens, and evidences, and signs. If you rest on the

finished work of Jesus you have already the best evidence of your salvation in the world! You have God's Word for it—what more is needed? Cannot you take God's Word? You can take your father's word. You can take your mother's word—why cannot you take God's word? Oh, what base hearts we must have to suspect God Himself!

Perhaps you say you would not do such a thing. Oh, but you doubt God, if you do not trust Christ—for, "he that believes not has made God a liar." If you do not trust Christ, you do in effect say that God is a liar! You do not want to say that, do you? Oh, believe the truthfulness of God! May the Spirit of God constrain you to believe the Father's mercy, the power of the Son's blood, and the willingness of the Holy Spirit to bring sinners to Himself!

Come, my dear hearers, join with me in the prayer that you may be led by divine grace to see in Jesus all that you need—

> "Prayer is a creature's strength, his very breath and being.
> Prayer is the golden key that can open the wicket of mercy.
> Prayer is the magic sound that said to fate, so be it.
> Prayer is the slender nerve that moves the muscles of
>   Omnipotence,
> Therefore, pray, O creature, for many and great are your
>   needs.
> Your mind, your conscience, and your being, your needs
>   commend you unto prayer,
> The cure of all cares, the grand panacea for all pains,
> Doubt's destroyer, ruin's remedy, the antidote to all
>   anxieties."

III. Order and Argument in Prayer

*Oh that I knew where I might find him! that I might
come even to his seat! I would order my cause before
him, and fill my mouth with arguments.*
Job 23:3,4

In Job's uttermost extremity he cried after the Lord. The
longing desire of an afflicted child of God is once more
to see his Father's face. His first prayer is not, "Oh that I
might be healed of the disease which now festers in every
part of my body!" nor even, "Oh that I might see my children restored from the jaws of the grave, and my property
once more brought from the hand of the spoiler!" but the
first and uppermost cry is, "Oh that I knew where I might
find Him—who is my God! that I might come even to his
seat!" God's children run home when the storm comes
on. It is the heaven-born instinct of a gracious soul to seek
shelter from all ills beneath the wings of Jehovah. "He that
hath made his refuge God," might serve as the title of a
true believer. A hypocrite, when he feels that he has been
afflicted by God, resents the infliction, and, like a slave,
would run from the master who has scourged him; but
not so the true heir of heaven, he kisses the hand which
smote him, and seeks shelter from the rod in the bosom of
that very God who frowned upon him. You will observe
that the desire to commune with God is intensified by the
failure of all other sources of consolation. When Job first
saw his friends at a distance, he may have entertained a
hope that their kindly counsel and compassionate tenderness would blunt the edge of his grief; but they had not
long spoken before he cried out in bitterness, "Miserable
comforters are ye all." They put salt into his wounds, they
heaped fuel upon the flame of his sorrow, they added the
gall of their upbraidings to the wormwood of his griefs.
In the sunshine of his smile they once had longed to sun
themselves, and now they dare to cast shadows upon his
reputation, most ungenerous and undeserved. Alas for a
man when his wine-cup mocks him with vinegar, and his

pillow pricks him with thorns! The patriarch turned away
from his sorry friends and looked up to the celestial throne,
just as a traveller turns from his empty skin bottle and be-
takes himself with all speed to the well. He bids farewell to
earthborn hopes, and cries, "Oh that I knew where I might
find my God!" My brethren, nothing teaches us so much
the preciousness of the Creator as when we learn the emp-
tiness of all besides. When you have been pierced through
and through with the sentence, "Cursed is he that trusteth
in man, and maketh flesh his arm," then will you suck un-
utterable sweetness from the divine assurance, "Blessed is
he that trusteth in the Lord, and whose hope the Lord is."
Turning away with bitter scorn from earth's hives, where
you found no honey, but many sharp stings, you will rejoice in him whose faithful word is sweeter than honey or
the honeycomb.

It is further observable that though a good man hastens
to God in his trouble, and runs with all the more speed because of the unkindness of his fellow men, yet sometimes
the gracious soul is left without the comfortable presence
of God. This is the worst of all griefs; the text is one of Job's
deep groans, far deeper than any which came from him on
account of the loss of his children and his property: "Oh
that I knew where I might find Him!" The worst of all losses is to lose the smile of my God. He now had a foretaste
of the bitterness of his Redeemer's cry, "My God, my God,
why hast thou forsaken me?" God's presence is always
with his people in one sense, so far as secretly sustaining
them is concerned, but his manifest presence they do not
always enjoy. Like the spouse in the song, they seek their
beloved by night upon their bed, they seek him but they
find him not; and though they wake and roam through
the city they may not discover him, and the question may
be sadly asked again and again, "Saw ye him whom my
soul loveth?" You may be beloved of God, and yet have
no consciousness of that love in your soul. You may be as
dear to his heart as Jesus Christ himself, and yet for a small
moment he may forsake you, and in a little wrath he may
hide himself from you. But, dear friends, at such times the
desire of the believing soul gathers yet greater intensity
from the fact of God's light being withheld. Instead of
saying with proud lip, "Well, if he leaveth me I must do
without him; if I cannot have his comfortable presence I
must fight on as best may be," the soul saith, "No, it is
my very life; I must have my God. I perish, I sink in deep

mire where there is no standing, and nothing but the arm of God can deliver me." The gracious soul addresseth itself with a double zeal to find out God, and sends up its groans, its entreaties, its sobs and sighs to heaven more frequently and fervently. "Oh that I knew where I might find him!" Distance or labour are as nothing; if the soul only knew where to go she would soon overleap the distance. She makes no stipulation about mountains or rivers, but vows that if she knew where, she would come even to his seat. My soul in her hunger would break through stone walls, or scale the battlements of heaven to reach her God, and though there were seven hells between me and him, yet would I face the flame if I might reach him, nothing daunted if I had but the prospect of at last standing in his presence and feeling the delight of his love. That seems to me to be the state of mind in which Job pronounced the words before us.

But we cannot stop upon this point, for the object of this morning's discourse beckons us onward. It appears that Job's end, in desiring the presence of God, was that he might pray to him. He had prayed, but he wanted to pray as in God's presence. He desired to plead as before one whom he knew would hear and help him. He longed to state his own case before the seat of the impartial Judge, before the very face of the all-wise God; he would appeal from the lower courts, where his friends judged unrighteous judgment, to the court of King's bench—the high court of Heaven—there, saith he, "I would order my cause before him, and fill my mouth with arguments."

In this latter verse Job teaches us how he meant to plead and intercede with God. He does, as it were, reveal the secrets of his closet, and unveils the art of prayer. We are here admitted into the guild of suppliants; we are shown the art and mystery of pleading; we have here taught to us the blessed handicraft and science of prayer, and if we can be bound apprentice to Job this morning, for the next hour, and can have a lesson from Job's Master, we may acquire no little skill in interceding with God.

There are two things here set forth as necessary in prayer—ordering of our cause, and filling our mouth with arguments. We shall speak of those two things, and then if we have rightly learned the lesson, a blessed result will follow.

I. First, it is needful that our suit be ordered before God.

There is a vulgar notion that prayer is a very easy thing, a kind of common business that may be done anyhow, without care or effort. Some think that you have only to reach a book down and get through a certain number of very excellent words, and you have prayed and may put the book up again; others suppose that to use a book is superstitious, and that you ought rather to repeat extemporaneous sentences, sentences which come to your mind with a rush, like a herd of swine or a pack of hounds, and that when you have uttered them with some little attention to what you have said, you have prayed. Now neither of these modes of prayer were adopted by ancient saints. They appear to have thought a great deal more seriously of prayer than many do now-a-days. It seems to have been a mighty business with them, a long-practised exercise, in which some of them attained great eminence, and were thereby singularly blest. They reaped great harvests in the field of prayer, and found the mercy seat to be a mine of untold treasures.

The ancient saints were wont, with Job, to order their cause before God; that is to say, as a petitioner coming into court does not come there without thought to state his case on the spur of the moment, but enters into the audience chamber with his suit well prepared, having moreover learned how he ought to behave himself in the presence of the great One to whom he is appealing. It is well to approach the seat of the King of kings as much as possible with premeditation and preparation, knowing what we are about, where we are standing, and what it is which we desire to obtain. In times of peril and distress we may fly to God just as we are, as the dove enters the cleft of the rock, even though her plumes are ruffled; but in ordinary times we should not come with an unprepared spirit, even as a child comes not to his father in the morning till he has washed his face. See yonder priest; he has a sacrifice to offer, but he does not rush into the court of the priests and hack at the bullock with the first pole-axe upon which he can lay his hand, but when he rises he washes his feet at the brazen laver, he puts on his garments, and adorns himself with his priestly vestments; then he comes to the altar with his victim properly divided according to the law, and is careful to do according to the command, even to such a simple matter as the placing of the fat, and the liver, and the kidneys, and he taketh the blood in a bowl and poureth it in an appropriate place at the foot of the

altar, not throwing it just as may occur to him, and kindles
the fire not with common flame, but with the sacred fire
from off the altar. Now this ritual is all superseded, but the
truth which it taught remains the same; our spiritual sacrifices should be offered with holy carefulness. God forbid
that our prayer should be a mere leaping out of one's bed
and kneeling down, and saying anything that comes first
to hand; on the contrary, may we wait upon the Lord with
holy fear and sacred awe. See how David prayed when
God had blessed him—he went in before the Lord. Understand that; he did not stand outside at a distance, but
he went in before the Lord and he sat down—for sitting
is not a bad posture for prayer, let who will speak against
it—and sitting down quietly and calmly before the Lord
he then began to pray, but not until first he had thought
over the divine goodness, and so attained to the spirit of
prayer. Then by the assistance of the Holy Ghost did he
open his mouth. Oh that we oftener sought the Lord in
this style! Abraham may serve us as a pattern; he rose up
early—here was his willingness; he went three days journey—here was his zeal; he left his servants at the foot of
the hill—here was his privacy; he carried the wood and
the fire with him—here was his preparation; and lastly, he
built the altar and laid the wood in order, and then took
the knife—here was the devout carefulness of his worship.
David puts it, "In the morning will I direct my prayer unto
thee, and will look up"; which I have frequently explained
to you to mean that he marshalled his thoughts like men
of war, or that he aimed his prayers like arrows. He did
not take the arrow and put it on the bowstring and shoot,
and shoot, and shoot anywhere; but after he had taken out
the chosen shaft, and fitted it to the string, he took delib-
erate aim. He looked—looked well—at the white of the
target; kept his eye fixed on it, directing his prayer, and
then drew his bow with all his strength and let the arrow
fly; and then, when the shaft had left his hand, what does
he say? "I will look up." He looked up to see where the
arrow went, to see what effect it had; for he expected an
answer to his prayers, and was not as many who scarcely
think of their prayers after they have uttered them. David knew that he had an engagement before him which
required all his mental powers; he marshalled up his fac-
ulties and went about the work in a workmanlike manner,
as one who believed in it and meant to succeed. We should
plough carefully and pray carefully. The better the work

the more attention it deserves. To be anxious in the shop and thoughtless in the closet is little less than blasphemy, for it is an insinuation that anything will do for God, but the world must have our best.

If any ask what order should be observed in prayer, I am not about to give you a scheme such as many have drawn out, in which adoration, confession, petition, intercession, and ascription are arranged in succession. I am not persuaded that any such order is of divine authority. It is to no mere mechanical order I have been referring, for our prayers will be equally acceptable, and possibly equally proper, in any form; for there are specimens of prayers, in all shapes, in the Old and New Testament. The true spiritual order of prayer seems to me to consist in something more than mere arrangement. It is most fitting for us first to feel that we are now doing something that is real; that we are about to address ourselves to God, whom we cannot see, but who is really present; whom we can neither touch nor hear, nor by our senses can apprehend, but who, nevertheless, is as truly with us as though we were speaking to a friend of flesh and blood like ourselves. Feeling the reality of God's presence, our mind will be led by divine grace into an humble state; we shall feel like Abraham, when he said, "I have taken upon myself to speak unto God, I that am but dust and ashes." Consequently we shall not deliver ourselves of our prayer as boys repeating their lessons, as a mere matter of rote, much less shall we speak as if we were rabbis instructing our pupils, or as I have heard some do, with the coarseness of a highwayman stopping a person on the road and demanding his purse of him; but we shall be humble yet bold petitioners, humbly importuning mercy through the Saviour's blood. We shall not have the reserve of a slave but the loving reverence of a child, yet not an impudent, impertinent child, but a teachable obedient child, honouring his Father, and therefore asking earnestly, but with deferential submission to his Father's will. When I feel that I am in the presence of God, and take my rightful position in that presence, the next thing I shall want to recognize will be that I have no right to what I am seeking, and cannot expect to obtain it except as a gift of grace, and I must recollect that God limits the channel through which he will give me mercy—he will give it to me through his dear Son. Let me put myself then under the patronage of the great Redeemer. Let me feel that now it is no longer I that speak but Christ that speaketh with me, and that while I plead, I plead his wounds, his life, his death, his blood, himself. This is truly getting into order.

The next thing is to consider what I am to ask for? It is most proper in prayer, to aim at great distinctness of supplication. There is much reason to complain of some public prayers, that those who offer them do not really ask God for anything. I must acknowledge I fear to having so prayed myself, and certainly to having heard many prayers of the kind, in which I did not feel that anything was sought for from God—a great deal of very excellent doctrinal and experimental matter uttered, but little real petitioning, and that little in a nebulous kind of state, chaotic and unformed. But it seems to me that prayer should be distinct, the asking for something definitely and distinctly because the mind has realized its distinct need of such a thing, and therefore must plead for it. It is well not to beat round the bush in prayer, but to come directly to the point. I like that prayer of Abraham's, "Oh that Ishmael might live before thee!" There is the name and the person prayed for, and the blessing desired, all put in a few words,—"Ishmael might live before thee!" Many persons would have used a roundabout expression of this kind, "Oh that our beloved offspring might be regarded with the favour which thou bearest to those who," etc. Say "Ishmael," if you mean "Ishmael"; put it in plain words before the Lord. Some people cannot even pray for the minister without using such circular descriptives that you might think it were the parish beadle,[5] or somebody whom it did not do to mention too particularly. Why not be distinct, and say what we mean as well as mean what we say? Ordering our cause would bring us to greater distinctness of mind. It is not necessary, my dear brethren, in the closet to ask for every supposable good thing; it is not necessary to rehearse the catalogue of every want that you may have, have had, can have, or shall have. Ask for what you now need, and, as a rule, keep to present need; ask for your daily bread—what you want now—ask for that. Ask for it plainly, as before God, who does not regard your fine expressions, and to whom your eloquence and oratory will be less than nothing and vanity. Thou art before the Lord; let thy words be few, but let thy heart be fervent.

You have not quite completed the ordering when you have asked for what you want through Jesus Christ. There

---

5   A minor parish official.

should be a looking round the blessing which you desire, to see whether it is assuredly a fitting thing to ask; for some prayers would never be offered if men did but think. A little reflection would show to us that some things which we desire were better let alone. We may, moreover, have a motive at the bottom of our desire which is not Christ-like, a selfish motive, which forgets God's glory and caters only for our own case and comfort. Now although we may ask for things which are for our profit, yet still we must never let our profit interfere in any way with the glory of God. There must be mingled with acceptable prayer the holy salt of submission to the divine will. I like Luther's saying, "Lord, I will have my will of thee at this time." "What!" say you, "Like such an expression as that?" I do, because of the next clause, which was, "I will have my will, for I know that my will is thy will." That is well spoken, Luther; but without the last words it would have been wicked presumption. When we are sure that what we ask for is for God's glory, then, if we have power in prayer, we may say, "I will not let thee go except thou bless me": we may come to close dealings with God, and like Jacob with the angel we may even put it to the wrestle and seek to give the angel the fall sooner than be sent away without the benediction. But we must be quite clear, before we come to such terms as those, that what we are seeking is really for the Master's honour.

Put these three things together, the deep spirituality which recognises prayer as being real conversation with the invisible God—much distinctness which is the reality of prayer, asking for what we know we want—and withal much fervency, believing the thing to be necessary, and therefore resolving to obtain it if it can be had by prayer, and above all these complete submission, leaving it still with the Master's will;—commingle all these, and you have a clear idea of what it is to order your cause before the Lord.

Still prayer itself is an art which only the Holy Ghost can teach us. He is the giver of all prayer. Pray for prayer—pray till you can pray; pray to be helped to pray, and give not up praying because thou canst not pray, for it is when thou thinkest thou canst not pray that thou art most praying; and sometimes when thou hast no sort of comfort in thy supplications, it is then that thy heart all broken and cast down is really wrestling and truly prevailing with the Most High.

II. The second part of prayer is filling the mouth with arguments—not filling the mouth with words nor good phrases, nor pretty expressions, but filling the mouth with arguments are the knocks of the rapper by which the gate is opened.

Why are arguments to be used at all? Is the first enquiry; the reply being, certainly not because God is slow to give, not because we can change the divine purpose, not because God needeth to be informed of any circumstance with regard to ourselves or of anything in connection with the mercy asked: the arguments to be used are for our own benefit, not for his. He requires for us to plead with him, and to bring forth our strong reasons, as Isaiah saith, because this will show that we feel the value of the mercy. When a man searches for arguments for a thing it is because he attaches importance to that which he is seeking. Again, our use of arguments teaches us the ground upon which we obtain the blessing. If a man should come with the argument of his own merit, he would never succeed; the successful argument is always founded upon grace, and hence the soul so pleading is made to understand intensely that it is by grace and by grace alone that a sinner obtaineth anything of the Lord. Besides, the use of arguments is intended to stir up our fervency. The man who uses one argument with God will get more force in using the next, and will use the next with still greater power, and the next with more force still. The best prayers I have ever heard in our prayer meetings have been those which have been fullest of argument. Sometimes my soul has been fairly melted down when I have listened to brethren who have come before God feeling the mercy to be really needed, and that they must have it, for they first pleaded with God to give it for this reason, and then for a second, and then for a third, and then for a fourth and a fifth, until they have awakened the fervency of the entire assembly. My brethren, there is no need for prayer at all as far as God is concerned, but what a need there is for it on our own account! If we were not constrained to pray, I question whether we could even live as Christians. If God's mercies came to us unasked, they would not be half so useful as they now are, when they have to be sought for; for now we get a double blessing, a blessing in the obtaining, and a blessing in the seeking. The very act of prayer is a blessing. To pray is as it were to bathe one's-self in a cool purling stream,[6] and so to escape from the heats of earth's summer sun. To pray is to mount on eagle's wings above the clouds and get into the clear heaven where God dwelleth. To pray is to enter the treasure-house of God and to enrich one's-self out of an inexhaustible storehouse. To pray is to grasp heaven in one's arms, to embrace the Deity within one's soul, and to feel one's body made a temple of the Holy Ghost. Apart from the answer prayer is in itself a benediction. To pray, my brethren, is to cast off your burdens, it is to tear away your rags, it is to shake off your diseases, it is to be filled with spiritual vigour, it is to reach the highest point of Christian health. God give us to be much in the holy art of arguing with God in prayer.

The most interesting part of our subject remains; it is a very rapid summary and catalogue of a few of the arguments which have been used with great success with God. I cannot give you a full list; that would require a treatise such as Master John Owen might produce. It is well in prayer to plead with Jehovah his attributes. Abraham did so when he laid hold upon God's justice. Sodom was to be pleaded for, and Abraham begins, "Peradventure there be fifty righteous within the city: wilt thou also destroy and not spare the place for the fifty righteous that are therein? that be far from thee to do after this manner, to slay the righteous with the wicked: and that the righteous should be as the wicked, that be far from thee: Shall not the Judge of all the earth do right?" Here the wrestling begins. It was a powerful argument by which the patriarch grasped the Lord's left hand, and arrested it just when the thunderbolt was about to fall. But there came a reply to it. It was intimated to him that this would not spare the city, and you notice how the good man, when sorely pressed, retreated by inches; and at last, when he could no longer lay hold upon justice, grasped God's right hand of mercy, and that gave him a wondrous hold when he asked that if there were but ten righteous there the city might be spared. So you and I may take hold at any time upon the justice, the mercy, the faithfulness, the wisdom, the long-suffering, the tenderness of God, and we shall find every attribute of the Most High to be, as it were, a great battering-ram, with which we may open the gates of heaven.

Another mighty piece of ordinance in the battle of prayer is God's promise. When Jacob was on the other side of the brook Jabbok, and his brother Esau was coming

---

6 A small flowing stream with a murmuring sound.

with armed men, he pleaded with God not to suffer Esau
to destroy the mother and the children, and as a master
reason he pleaded, "And thou saidst, surely I will do thee
good." Oh the force of that plea! He was holding God to
his word: "Thou saidst." The attribute is a splendid horn
of the altar to lay hold upon; but the promise, which has in
it the attribute and something more, is yet a mightier holdfast. "Thou saidst." Remember how David put it. After
Nathan had spoken the promise, David said at the close
of his prayer, "Do as thou hast said." That is a legitimate
argument with every honest man, and has he said, and
shall he not do it? "Let God be true, and every man a liar."
Shall not he be true? Shall he not keep his word? Shall not
every word that cometh out of his lips stand fast and be
fulfilled? Solomon, at the opening of the temple, used this
same mighty plea. He pleads with God to remember the
word which he had spoken to his father David, and to
bless that place. When a man gives a promissory note his
honour is engaged. He signs his hand, and he must dis-
charge it when the due time comes, or else he loses credit.
It shall never be said that God dishonours his bills. The
credit of the Most High never was impeached, and never
shall be. He is punctual to the moment; he never is before
his time, but he never is behind it. You shall search this
Book through, and you shall compare it with the experience of God's people, and the two tally from the first to
the last; and many a hoary patriarch has said with Joshua
in his old age, "Not one good thing hath failed of all that
the Lord God hath promised: all hath come to pass." My
brother, if you have a divine promise, you need not plead
it with an "if" in it; you may plead with a certainty. If for
the mercy which you are now asking, you have God's sol-
emnly pledged word, there will scarce be any room for the
caution about submission to his will. You know his will:
that will is in the promise; plead it. Do not give him rest
until he fulfil it. He meant to fulfil it, or else he would not
have given it. God does not give his words merely to quiet our noise, and to keep us hopeful for awhile, with the
intention of putting us off at last; but when he speaks, he
speaks because he means to act.

A third argument to be used is that employed by Moses, the great name of God. How mightily did he argue
with God on one occasion upon this ground! "What wilt
thou do for thy great name? The Egyptians will say, Because the Lord could not bring them into the land, there-

fore he slew them in the wilderness." There are some occasions when the name of God is very closely tied up with
the history of his people. Sometimes in reliance upon a divine promise, a believer will be led to take a certain course
of action. Now, if the Lord should not be as good as his
promise, not only is the believer deceived, but the wicked world looking on would say, "Aha! aha! Where is your
God?" Take the case of our respected brother, Mr. Muller,
of Bristol. These many years he has declared that God
hears prayer, and firm in that conviction, he has gone on
to build house after house for the maintenance of orphans.
Now, I can very well conceive that, if he were driven to a
point of want of means for the maintenance of those thousand or two thousand children, he might very well use the
plea, "What wilt thou do for thy great name?" And you,
in some severe trouble, when you have fairly received the
promise, may say, "Lord, thou hast said, 'In six troubles
I will be with thee, and in seven I will not forsake thee.' I
have told my friends and neighbours that I put my trust
in thee, and if thou do not deliver me now, where is thy
name? Arise, O God, and do this thing, lest thy honour be
cast into the dust." Coupled with this, we may employ the
further argument of the hard things said by the revilers.
It was well done of Hezekiah, when he took Rabshakeh's
letter and spread it before the Lord. Will that help him? It
is full of blasphemy, will that help him? "Where are the
gods of Arphad and Sepharvaim? Where are the gods
of the cities which I have overthrown? Let not Hezekiah
deceive you, saying that Jehovah will deliver you." Does
that have any effect? Oh! yes, it was a blessed thing that
Rabshakeh wrote that letter, for it provoked the Lord to
help his people. Sometimes the child of God can rejoice
when he sees his enemies get thoroughly out of temper
and take to reviling. "Now," he says, "they have reviled
the Lord himself; not me alone have they assailed, but the
Most High himself. Now it is no longer the poor insignificant Hezekiah with his little band of soldiers, but it is Jehovah, the King of angels, who has come to fight against
Rabshakeh. Now what wilt thou do, O boastful soldier of
proud Sennacherib? Shalt not thou be utterly destroyed,
since Jehovah himself has come into the fray? All the prog-
ress that is made by Popery, all the wrong things said by
speculative atheists and so on, should be by Christians
used as an argument with God, why he should help the
gospel. Lord; see how they reproach the gospel of Jesus!

Pluck thy right hand out of thy bosom! O God, they defy thee! Anti-christ thrusts itself into the place where thy Son once was honoured, and from the very pulpits where the gospel was once preached Popery is now declared. Arise, O God, wake up thy zeal, let thy sacred passions burn! Thine ancient foe again prevails. Behold the harlot of Babylon once more upon her scarlet-coloured beast rides forth in triumph! Come, Jehovah, come, Jehovah, and once again show what thy bare arm can do!" This is a legitimate mode of pleading with God, for his great name's sake.

So also may we plead the sorrows of his people. This is frequently done. Jeremiah is the great master of this art. He says, "Her Nazarites were purer than snow, they were whiter than milk, they were more ruddy in body than rubies, their polishing was of sapphire: their visage is blacker than a coal." "The precious sons of Zion, comparable to fine gold, how are they esteemed as earthen pitchers, the work of the hands of the potter!" He talks of all their griefs and straitnesses in the siege. He calls upon the Lord to look upon his suffering Zion; and ere long his plaintive cries are heard. Nothing so eloquent with the father as his child's cry; yes, there is one thing more mighty still, and that is a moan,—when the child is so sick that it is past crying, and lies moaning with that kind of moan which indicates extreme suffering and intense weakness. Who can resist that moan? Ah! and when God's Israel shall be brought very low so that they can scarcely cry but only their moans are heard, then comes the Lord's time of deliverance, and he is sure to show that he loveth his people. Dear friends, whenever you also are brought into the same condition you may plead your moanings, and when you see a church brought very low you may use her griefs as an argument why God should return and save the remnant of his people.

Brethren, it is good to plead with God the past. Ah, you experienced people of God, you know how to do this. Here is David's specimen of it: "Thou hast been my help. Leave me not, neither forsake me." He pleads God's mercy to him from his youth up. He speaks of being cast upon his God from his very birth, and then he pleads, "Now also, when I am old and grey-headed, O God, forsake me not." Moses also, speaking with God, says, "Thou didst bring this people up out of Egypt." As if he would say, "Do not leave thy work unfinished; thou hast begun to build, complete it. Thou hast fought the first battle; Lord, end

the campaign! Go on till thou gettest a complete victory."
How often have we cried in our trouble, "Lord, thou didst
deliver me in such and such a sharp trial, when it seemed
as if no help were near; thou hast never forsaken me yet.
I have set up my Ebenezer in thy name. If thou hadst intended to leave me why hast thou showed me such things?
Hast thou brought thy servant to this place to put him to
shame?" Brethren, we have to deal with an unchanging
God, who will do in the future what he has done in the
past, because he never turns from his purpose, and cannot
be thwarted in his design; the past thus becomes a very
mighty means of winning blessings from him.

We may even use our own unworthiness as an argument with God. "Out of the eater comes forth meat, and
out of the strong comes forth sweetness." David in one
place pleads thus: "Lord, have mercy upon mine iniquity,
for it is great." That is a very singular mode of reasoning;
but being interpreted it means, "Lord, why shouldest thou
go about doing little things? Thou art a great God, and
here is a great sinner. Here is a fitness in me for the display
of thy grace. The greatness of my sin makes me a platform
for the greatness of thy mercy. Let the greatness of thy love
be seen in me." Moses seems to have the same on his mind
when he asks God to show his great power in sparing his
sinful people. The power with which God restrains himself
is great indeed. O brothers and sisters, there is such a thing
as creeping down at the foot of the throne, crouching low
and crying, "O God, break me not—I am a bruised reed.
Oh! tread not on my little life, it is now but as the smok-
ing flax. Wilt thou hunt me? Wilt thou come out, as David
said, 'after a dead dog, after a flea?' Wilt thou pursue me
as a leaf that is blown in the tempest? Wilt thou watch me,
as Job saith, as though I were a vast sea, or a great whale?
Nay, but because I am so little, and because the greatness
of thy mercy can be shown in one so insignificant and yet
so vile, therefore, O God, have mercy upon me."

There was once an occasion when the very Godhead
of Jehovah made a triumphant plea for the prophet Elijah.
On that august occasion, when he had bidden his adversaries see whether their god could answer them by fire,
you can little guess the excitement there must have been
that day in the prophet's mind. With what stern sarcasm
did he say, "Cry aloud: for he is a god; either he is talking,
or he is pursuing, or he is in a journey, or peradventure he
sleepeth, and must be awakened." And as they cut them-

selves with knives, and leaped upon the altar, oh the scorn with which that man of God must have looked down upon their impotent exertions, and their earnest but useless cries! But think of how his heart must have palpitated, if it had not been for the strength of his faith, when he repaired the altar of God that was broken down, and laid the wood in order, and killed the bullock. Hear him cry, "Pour water on it. You shall not suspect me of concealing fire; pour water on the victim." When they had done so, he bids them, "Do it a second time"; and they did it a second time; and then he says, "Do it a third time." And when it was all covered with water, soaked and saturated through, then he stands up and cries to God, "O God, let it be known that thou only art God." Here everything was put to the test. Jehovah's own existence was now put, as it were, at stake, before the eyes of men by this bold prophet. But how well the prophet was heard! Down came the fire and devoured not only the sacrifice, but even the wood, and the stones, and even the very water that was in the trenches, for Jehovah God had answered his servant's prayer. We sometimes may do the same, and say unto him, "Oh, by thy Deity, by thine existence, if indeed thou be God, now show thyself for the help of thy people!"

Lastly, the grand Christian argument is the sufferings, the death, the merit, the intercession of Christ Jesus. Brethren, I am afraid we do not understand what it is that we have at our command when we are allowed to plead with God for Christ's sake. I met with this thought the other day: it was somewhat new to me, but I believe it ought not to have been. When we ask God to hear us, pleading Christ's name, we usually mean, "O Lord, thy dear Son deserves this of thee; do this unto me because of what he merits." But if we knew it we might go in the city, "Sir, call at my office, and use my name, and say that they are to give you such a thing." I should go in and use your name, and I should obtain my request as a matter of right and a matter of necessity. This is virtually what Jesus Christ says to us. "If you need anything of God, all that the Father has belongs to me; go and use my name." Suppose you should give a man your cheque-book signed with your own name and left blank, to be filled up as he chose; that would be very nearly what Jesus has done in these words, "If ye ask anything in my name, I will give it you." If I had a good name at the bottom of the cheque, I should be sure that I should get it cashed when I went to the banker with it;

so when you have got Christ's name, to whom the very justice of God hath become a debtor, and whose merits have claims with the Most High, when you have Christ's name there is no need to speak with fear and trembling and bated breath. Oh, waver not and let not faith stagger! When thou pleadest the name of Christ thou pleadest that which shakes the gates of hell, and which the hosts of heaven obey, and God himself feels the sacred power of that divine plea.

Brethren, you would do better if you sometimes thought more in your prayers of Christ's griefs and groans. Bring before the Lord his wounds, tell the Lord of his cries, make the groans of Jesus cry again from Gethsemane, and his blood speak again from that frozen Calvary. Speak out and tell the Lord that with such griefs, and cries, and groans to plead, thou canst not take a denial: such arguments as these will speed you.

III. If the Holy Ghost shall teach us how to order our cause, and how to fill our mouth with arguments, the result shall be that we shall have our mouth filled with praises. The man who has his mouth full of arguments in prayer shall soon have his mouth full of benedictions in answer to prayer. Dear friend, thou hast thy mouth full this morning, has thou? What of? Full of complaining? Pray the Lord to rinse thy mouth out of that black stuff, for it will little avail thee, and it will be bitter in thy bowels one of these days. Oh, have thy mouth full of prayer, full of it, full of arguments so that there is room for nothing else. Then come with this blessed mouthful, and you shall soon go away with whatsoever you have asked of God. Only delight thou thyself in him, and he will give thee the desire of thy heart.

It is said—I know not how truly—that the explanation of the text, "Open thy mouth wide and I will fill it," may be found in a very singular Oriental custom. It is said that not many years ago—I remember the circumstance being reported—the King of Persia ordered the chief of his nobility, who had done something or other which greatly gratified him, to open his mouth, and when he had done so he began to put into his mouth pearls, diamonds, rubies, and emeralds, till he had filled it as full as it could hold, and then he bade him go his way. This is said to have been occasionally done in Oriental courts towards great favourites. Now certainly whether that be an explanation of the text or not it is an illustration of it. God says, "Open thy mouth with arguments," and then he will fill it with mercies priceless, gems unspeakably valuable. Would not a man open his mouth wide when he had to have it filled in such a style? Surely the most simple-minded among you would be wise enough for that. Oh! let us then open wide our mouth when we have to plead with God. Our needs are great, let our askings be great, and the supply shall be great too. You are not straitened in him; you are straitened in your own bowels. The Lord give you large mouths in prayer, great potency, not in the use of language, but in employing arguments.

What I have been speaking to the Christian is applicable in great measure to the unconverted man. God give thee to see the force of it, and to fly in humble prayer to the Lord Jesus Christ and to find eternal life in him.

IV. Pleading

*But I am poor and needy: make haste unto me, O
God: Thou art my help and my deliverer; O Lord,
make no tarrying.*
Psalm 70:5

Young painters were anxious, in olden times, to study under the great masters. They concluded that they should
more easily attain to excellence if they entered the schools
of eminent men. Men have paid large premiums that their
sons may be apprenticed or articled to those who best
understood their trades or professions; now, if any of us
would learn the sacred art and mystery of prayer, it is well
for us to study the productions of the greatest masters of
that science. I am unable to point out one who understood
it better than did the psalmist David. So well did he know
how to praise, that his psalms have become the language
of good men in all ages; and so well did he understand
how to pray, that if we catch his spirit, and follow his
mode of prayer, we shall have learned to plead with God
after the most prevalent sort. Place before you, first of all,
David's Son and David's Lord, that most mighty of all in-
tercessors, and, next to Him, you shall find David to be
one of the most admirable models for your imitation.

We shall consider our text, then, as one of the productions of a great master in spiritual matters, and we will
study it, praying all the while that God will help us to pray
after the like fashion.

In our text we have the soul of a successful pleader
under four aspects: we view, first, the soul confessing: "I
am poor and needy." You have next, the soul pleading,
for he makes a plea out of his poor condition, and adds,
"Make haste unto me, O God!" You see, thirdly, a soul in
it's urgency, for he cries, "Make haste," and he varies the
expression but keeps the same idea: "Make no tarrying."
And you have in the fourth and last view, a soul grasping
God, for the psalmist puts it thus: "Thou art my help and
my deliverer"; thus with both hands he lays hold upon

49

His God, so as not to let Him go till a blessing is obtained.

I. To begin with, then, we see in this model of supplication, a soul confessing. The wrestler strips before he
enters upon the contest, and confession does the like for
the man who is about to plead with God. A racer on the
plains of prayer cannot hope to win, unless, by confession,
repentance, and faith, he lays aside every weight of sin.

Now, let it be ever remembered that confession is ab-
solutely needful to the sinner when he first seeks a saviour. It is not possible for thee, O seeker, to obtain peace
for thy troubled heart, till thou shalt have acknowledged
thy transgression and thine iniquity before the Lord. Thou
mayest do what thou wilt, ay, even attempt to believe in
Jesus, but thou shalt find that the faith of God's elect is
not in thee, unless thou art willing to make a full confession of thy transgression, and lay bare thy heart before
God. We do not usually think of giving charity to those
who do not acknowledge that they need it: the physician
does not send his medicine to those who are not sick. The
blind man in the gospels had to feel his blindness, and to
sit by the wayside begging; if he had entertained a doubt
as to whether he were blind of not, the Lord would have
passed him by. He opens the eyes of those who confess
their blindness, but of others, He says, "Because ye say we
see, therefore, your sin remaineth." He asks of those who
are brought to Him, "What wilt thou that I should do unto
thee?" in order that their need may be publicly avowed. It
must be so with all of us: we must offer the confession, or
we cannot gain the benediction.

Let me speak especially to you who desire to find
peace with God, and salvation through the precious blood:
you will do well to make your confession before God very
frank, very sincere, very explicit. Surely you have nothing
to hide, for there is nothing that you can hide. He knows
your guilt already, but He would have you know it, and
therefore He bids you confess it. Go into the details of your
sin in your secret acknowledgments before God; strip
yourself of all excuses, make no apologies; say, "Against
thee, thee only have I sinned, and done this evil in thy
sight: that thou mightest be justified when thou speakest,
and be clear when thou judgest." Acknowledge the evil of
sin, ask God to make you feel it; do not treat it as a trifle,
for it is none. To redeem the sinner from the effect of sin
Christ Himself must needs die, and unless you be deliv-
ered from it you must die eternally. Therefore, play not

with sin; do not confess it as though it were some venial
fault, which would not have been noticed unless God had
been too severe; but labour to see sin as God sees it, as an
offence against all that is good, a rebellion against all that
is kind; see it to be treason, to be ingratitude, or be a mean
and base thing. Do not think that you can improve your
condition before God by painting your case in brighter co-
lours than it should be. Blacken it: if it were possible black-
en it, but it is not possible. When you feel your sin most
you have not half felt it; when you confess it most fully
you do not know a tithe of it; but oh, to the utmost of your
ability make a clean breast of it, and say, "I have sinned
against heaven, and before thee." Acknowledge the sins of
your youth and your manhood, the sins of your body and
of your soul, the sins of omission and of commission, sins
against the law and offenses against the gospel; acknowledge all; neither for a moment seek to deny one portion of
the evil with which God's law, your own conscience, and
his Holy Spirit justly charge you.

And oh, soul, if thou wouldst get peace and approval
with God in prayer, confess the ill desert of thy sin. Submit
thyself to do whatever divine justice may sentence thee
to endure: confess that the deepest hell is thy desert, and
confess this not with thy lips only, but with thy soul. Let
this be the doleful ditty of thine inmost heart—

>"Should sudden vengeance seize my breath,
>I must pronounce thee just in death
>And, if my soul were sent to hell,
>Thy righteous law approves it well."

If thou wilt condemn thyself, God will acquit thee; if
thou wilt put the rope about thy neck, and sentence thyself, then he who otherwise would have sentenced thee
will say, "I forgive thee, through the merit of my son."
But never expect that the King of heaven will pardon a
traitor, if he will not confess and forsake his treason. Even
the tenderest father expects that the child should humble
himself when he has offended, and will not withdraw his
frown from him till with tears he has said, "Father, I have
sinned." Darest thou expect God to humble Himself to
thee, and would it not be so if He did not constrain thee to
humble thyself to Him? Wouldst thou have Him connive
at thy faults and wink at thy transgressions? He will have
mercy, but He must be holy. He is ready to forgive, but
not to tolerate sin; and, therefore, He cannot let thee be

forgiven if thou huggest thy sins, or if thou presumest to say, "I have not sinned." Hasten, then, O seeker, hasten I pray thee, to the mercy seat with this upon thy lips: "I am poor and needy, I am sinful, I am lost; have pity on me." With such an acknowledgment thou beginnest thy prayer well, and through Jesus thou shalt prosper in it.

Beloved hearers, the same principle applies to the church of God. We are praying for a display of the Holy Spirit's power in this church, and, in order to successful pleading in this matter, it is necessary that we should unanimously make the confession of our text, "I am poor and needy." We must own that we are powerless in this business. Salvation is of the Lord and we cannot save a single soul. The Spirit of God is treasured up in Christ, and we must seek Him of the great head of the church. We cannot command the Spirit, and yet we can do nothing without Him. He bloweth where He listeth.[7] We must deeply feel and honestly acknowledge this. Will you not heartily assent to it my brethren and sisters at this hour. May I not ask you unanimously to renew the confession this morning? We must also acknowledge that we are not worthy that the Holy Spirit should condescend to work with us and by us. There is no fitness in us for his purposes, except he shall give us that fitness. Our sins might well provoke him to leave us: he has striven with us, he has been tender towards us, but he might well go away and say, "I will no more shine upon that church, and no more bless that ministry." Let us feel our unworthiness, it will be a good preparation for earnest prayer; for mark you, brethren, God will have His church before He blesses it know that the blessing is altogether from Himself. "Not by might nor by power, but by my Spirit, saith the Lord." The career of Gideon was a very remarkable one, and it commenced with two most instructive signs. I think our heavenly Father would have all of us learn the very same lesson which He taught to Gideon, and when we have mastered that lesson, He will use us for His own purposes. You remember Gideon laid a fleece upon the barn floor, and in the morning all round was dry and the fleece alone was wet. God alone had saturated the fleece so that he could wring it out, and its moisture was not due to its being placed in a favourable situation, for all around was dry. He would have us learn, that, if the dew of His grace fills any one of us with its heavenly moisture, it is not be-

---

7   Wills, wishes.

cause we lie upon the barn-floor of a ministry which God usually blesses, or because we are in a church which the Lord graciously visits; but we must be made to see that the visitations of His Spirit are fruits of the Lord's sovereign grace, and gifts of His infinite love, and not of the will of man, neither by man. But then the miracle was reversed, for, as old Thomas Fuller says, "God's miracles will bear to be turned inside out and look as glorious one way as another." The next night the fleece was dry and all around was wet. For sceptics might have said, "Yes, but a fleece would naturally attract moisture, and if there were any in the air, it would be likely to be absorbed by the wool." But, lo, on this occasion, the dew is not where it might be expected to be, even though it lies thickly all around. Damp is the stone and dry is the fleece. So God will have us know that He does not give us His grace because of any natural adaptation in us to receive it, and even where He has given a preparedness of heart to receive, He will have us understand that His grace and His Spirit are most free in action, and sovereign in operation: and that He is not bound to work after any rule of our making. If the fleece be wet He bedews[8] it, and that not because it is a fleece, but because He chooses to do so. He will have all the glory of all His grace from first to last. Come then, my brethren, and become disciples to this truth. Consider that from the great Father of lights every good and perfect gift must come. We are His workmanship, he must work all our works in us.[9] Grace is not to be commanded by our position or condition: the wind bloweth where it listeth, the Lord works and no man can hinder; but if He works not, the mightiest and most zealous labour is but in vain.

It is very significant that before Christ fed the thousands, He made the disciples sum up all their provisions. It was well to let them see how low the commissariat had become, for then when the crowds were fed they could not say the basket fed them nor that the lad had done it. God will make us feel how little are our barley loaves, and how small our fishes, and compel us to enquire, "What are they among so many?" When the Saviour bade His disciples cast the net on the right side of the ship, and they dragged such a mighty shoal to land, He did not work the miracle till they had confessed that they had toiled all the

---

8   To cover or sprinkle with drops of water or other liquid.

9   Isaiah 26:12

night and had taken nothing. They were thus taught that the success of their fishery was dependent upon the Lord, and that it was not their net, nor the way of dragging it, nor their skill and art in handling their vessels, but that altogether and entirely their success came from their Lord. We must get down to this, and the sooner we come to it the better.

Before the ancient Jews kept the passover, observe what they did. The unleavened bread is to be brought in, and the paschal lamb to be eaten; but there shall be no unleavened bread and no paschal lamb, till they have purged out the old leaven. If you have any old strength and self-confidence; if you have anything that is your own, and is, therefore, leavened, it must be swept right out; there must be a bare cupboard before there can come in the heavenly provision, upon which the spiritual passover can be kept. I thank God when He clears us out; I bless His name when He brings us to feel our soul poverty as a church, for then the blessing will be sure to come.

One other illustration will show this, perhaps, more distinctly still. Behold Elijah with the priests of Baal at Carmel. The test appointed to decide Israel's choice was this—the God that answereth by fire let him be God. Baal's priests invoked the heavenly flame in vain. Elijah is confident that it will come upon his sacrifice, but he is also sternly resolved that the false priests and the fickle people shall not imagine that he himself had produced the fire. He determines to make it clear that there is no human contrivance, trickery, or maneuver about the matter. The flame should be seen to be of the Lord, and of the Lord alone. Remember the stern prophet's command, "Fill four barrels with water, and pour it on the burnt sacrifice, and on the wood. And he said, Do it a second time; and they did it a second time. And he said, Do it a third time; and they did it a third time. And the water ran round about the altar; and he filled the trench also with water." There could be no latent fire there. If there had been any combustibles or chemicals calculated to produce fire after the manner of the cheats of the time, they would all have been damped and spoiled. When no one could imagine that man could burn the sacrifice, then the prophet lifted up his eyes to heaven, and began to plead, and down came the fire of the Lord, which consumed the burnt sacrifice and the wood, and the altar stones and the dust, and even licked up the water that was in the trench. Then when all the people saw

it they fell on their faces, and they said, "Jehovah is the
God; Jehovah is the God." The Lord in this church, if He
means greatly to bless us, may send us trial of pouring on
the water once, and twice, and thrice; He may discourage
us, grieve us, and try us, and bring us low, till all shall see
that it is not of the preacher, it is not of the organization,
it is not of man, but altogether of God, the Alpha and the
Omega, who workest all things according to the council
of His will.

Thus I have shown you that for a successful season of
prayer the best beginning is confession that we are poor
and needy.

II. Secondly, after the soul has unburdened itself of
all weights of merit and self-sufficiency, it proceeds to
prayer, and we have before us a soul pleading. "I am poor
and needy, make haste unto me, O God. Thou art my help
and my deliverer: O Lord, make no tarrying." The careful
reader will perceive four pleas in this single verse.

Upon this topic I would remark that it is the habit
of faith, when she is praying, to use pleas. Mere prayer
sayers, who do not pray at all, forget to argue with God;
but those who would prevail bring forth their reasons
and their strong arguments and they debate the question
with the Lord. They who play at wrestling catch here and
there at random, but those who are really wrestling have a
certain way of grasping the opponent—a certain mode of
throwing, and the like; they work according to order and
rule. Faith's art of wrestling is to plead with God, and say
with holy boldness, "Let it be thus and thus, for these reasons." Hosea tells us of Jacob at Jabbok, "that there he spa-
ke with us"; from which I understand that Jacob instructed
us by his example. Now, the two pleas which Jacob used
were God's precept and God's promise. First, he said,
"Thou saidst unto me, Return unto thy country and to thy
kindred": as much as if he put it thus:—"Lord, I am in difficulty, but I have come here through obedience to thee.
Thou didst tell me to come hither, into the very teeth of
my brother Esau, who comes to meet me like a lion, Lord,
Thou canst not be so unfaithful as to bring me into danger
and then leave me in it." This was sound reasoning, and
it prevailed with God. Then Jacob also urged a promise:
"Thou saidst, I will surely do thee good." Among men, it
is a masterly way of reasoning when you can challenge
you opponent with his own words: you may quote other authorities, and he may say, "I deny their force"' but,

when you quote a man against himself, you foil him completely. When you bring a man's promise to his mind, he must either confess himself to be unfaithful and changeable, or if he holds to being the same, and being true to his word, you have him, and you have won your will of him. Oh brethren, let us learn thus to plead the precepts, the promises, and whatever else may serve our turn; but let us always have something to plead. Do not reckon you have prayed unless you have pleaded, for pleading is the very marrow of prayer. He who pleads well knows the secret of prevailing with God, especially if he pleads the blood of Jesus, for that unlocks the treasury of heaven. Many keys fit many locks, but the master-key is the blood and the name of Him that died but rose again, and ever lives in heaven to save unto the uttermost.

Faith's pleas are plentiful, and this is well, for faith is placed in diverse positions, and needs them all. She hath many needs, and having a keen eye she perceives that there are pleas to be urged in every case. I will not, therefore, tell you all faith's pleas, but I will just mention some of them, enough to let you see how abundant they are. Faith will plead all the attributes of God. "Thou art just, therefore spare thou the soul for whom the Saviour died. Thou art merciful, blot out my transgressions. Thou art good, reveal thy bounty to thy servant. Thou art immutable—thou hast done thus and thus to others of thy servants, do thus unto me. Thou art faithful, canst thou break thy promise, canst thou turn away from thy covenant?" Rightly viewed, all the perfections of Deity become pleas for faith.

Faith will boldly plead all God's gracious relationships. She will say to Him, "Art Thou not the creator? Wilt Thou forsake the work of thine own hands? Art Thou not the Redeemer, Thou hast redeemed thy servant, wilt Thou cast me away?" Faith usually delights to lay hold upon the fatherhood of God. This is generally one of her master points: when she brings this into the field she wins the day. "Thou art a Father, and wouldst Thou chasten us [as] though thou wouldst kill? A Father, and hast Thou no sympathy and no bowels of compassion? A Father, and canst Thou deny what Thine own child asks of Thee?" Whenever I am impressed with the divine majesty, and so, perhaps, a little dispirited in prayer, I find the short and sweet remedy is to remember that, although He is a great King, and infinitely glorious, I am His child, and no matter who the father is, the child may always be bold with his

father. Yes, faith can plead any and all of the relationships
in which God stands to His chosen.

Faith too, can ply heaven with the divine promises.
If you were to go to one of the banks in Lombard Street,
and see a man go in and out and lay a piece of paper on
the tables and take it up again and nothing more; if he did
that several times a day, I think there would soon be orders issued to the porter to keep the man out, because he
was merely wasting the clerk's time, and doing nothing
to purpose. Those city men who come to the bank in earnest present their cheques, they wait till they receive their
money and then they go, but not without having transact-
ed real business. They do not put the paper down, speak
about the excellent signature and discuss the correctness
of the document, but they want their money for it, and
they are not content without it. These are the people who
are always welcome at the bank, and not the triflers. Alas,
a great many people play at praying, it is nothing better.
I say they play at praying, they do not expect God to give
them an answer, and thus they are mere triflers, who mock
the Lord. He who prays in a businesslike way, meaning
what he says, honours the Lord. The Lord does not play at
promising, Jesus did not sport at confirming the word by
His blood, and we must not make a jest of prayer by going
about it in a listless unexpecting spirit. The Holy Spirit is
in earnest, and we must be in earnest also. We must go for
a blessing, and not be satisfied till we have it; like the hunt-
er, who is not satisfied because he has run so many miles,
but is never content till he takes his prey.

Faith, moreover, pleads the performances of God, she
looks back on the past and says, "Lord, thou didst deliver
me on such and such an occasion; wilt thou fail me now?"
She, moreover, takes her life as a whole, and pleads thus:—

> "After so much mercy past,
> Wilt thou let me sink at last?"

"Hast thou brought me so far that I may be put to
shame at the end?" She knows how to bring the ancient
mercies of God, and make them arguments for present favours. But your time would all be gone if I tried to exhibit,
even a thousandth part of faith's pleas.

Sometimes, however, faith's pleas are very singular.
As in this text, it is by no means according to the proud
rule of human nature to plead: "I am poor and needy,
make haste unto me, O God." It is like another prayer of

David: "Have mercy upon mine iniquity, for it is great." It is not the manner of men to plead so, they say, "Lord, have mercy on me, for I am not so bad a sinner as some." But faith reads things in a truer light, and bases her pleas on truth. "Lord, because my sin is great, and thou art a great God, let Thy great mercy be magnified in me." You know the story of the Syrophenician woman; that is a grand instance of the ingenuity of faith's reasoning. She came to Christ about her daughter, and He answered her not a word. What do you think her heart said? Why, she said in herself, "It is well, for He has not denied me: since He has not spoken at all, He has not refused me." With this for an encouragement, she began to plead again. Presently Christ spoke to her sharply, and then her brave heart said, "I have gained words from Him at last, I shall have deeds from Him by-and-by." That also cheered her; and then, when He called her a dog. "Ah," she reasoned, "but a dog is a part of the family, it has some connection with the master of the house. Though it does not eat meat from the table, it gets the crumbs under it, and so I have thee now, great Master, dog as I am; the great mercy that I ask of Thee, great as it is to me, is only a crumb to Thee; grant it then I beseech Thee." Could she fail to have her request? Impossible! When faith hath a will, she always finds a way, and she will win the day when all things forebode defeat.

Faith's pleas are singular, but, let me add, faith's pleas are always sound; for after all, it is a very telling plea to urge that we are poor and needy. Is not that the main argument with mercy? Necessity is the very best plea with benevolence, either human or divine. Is not our need the best reason we can urge? If we would have a physician come quickly to a sick man, "Sir," we say, "it is no common case, he is on the point of death, come to him, come quickly!" If we wanted our city firemen to rush to a fire, we should not say to them, "Make haste, for it is only a small fire"; but, on the contrary, we urge that it is an old house full of combustible materials, and there are rumours of petroleum and gunpowder on the premises; besides, it is near a timber yard, hosts of wooden cottages are close by, and before long we shall have half the city in a blaze." We put the case as bad as we can. Oh for wisdom to be equally wise in pleading with God, to find arguments everywhere, but especially to find them in our necessities.

They said two centuries ago that the trade of beggary was the easiest one to carry on, but it paid the worst. I am not sure about the last at this time, but certainly the trade of begging with God is a hard one, and undoubtedly it pays the best of anything in the world. It is very noteworthy that beggars with men have usually plenty of pleas on hand. When a man is hardly driven and starving, he can usually find a reason why he should ask aid of every likely person. Suppose it is a person to whom he is already under many obligations, then the poor creature argues, "I may safely ask of him again, for he knows me, and has been always very kind." If he never asked of the person before, then he says, "I have never worried him before; he cannot say he has already done all he can for me; I will make bold to begin with him." If it is one of his own kin, then he will say, "Surely you will help me in my distress, for you are a relation"; and if it be a stranger, he says, "I have often found strangers kinder than my own blood, help me, I entreat you." If he asks of the rich, he pleads that they will never miss what they give; and if he begs of the poor, he urges that they know what want means, and he is sure they will sympathize with him in his great distress. Oh that we were half as much on the alert to fill our mouths with arguments when we are before the Lord. How is it that we are not half awake, and do not seem to have any spiritual senses aroused. May God grant that we may learn the art of pleading with the eternal God, for in that shall rest our prevalence with Him, through the merit of Jesus Christ.

III. I must be brief on the next point. It is a soul urgent: "Make haste unto me, O God. O Lord, make no tarrying." We may well be urgent with God, if as yet we are not saved, for our need is urgent; we are in constant peril, and the peril is of the most tremendous kind. O sinner, within an hour, within a minute, thou mayest be where hope can never visit thee; therefore, cry, "Make haste, O God, to deliver me: make haste to help me, O Lord!" Yours is not a case that can bear lingering: you have not time to procrastinate; therefore, be urgent, for your need is so. And, remember, if you really are under a sense of need, and the Spirit of God is at work with you, you will and must be urgent. An ordinary sinner may be content to wait, but a quickened sinner wants mercy now. A dead sinner will lie quiet, but a living sinner cannot rest till pardon is sealed home to his soul. If you are urgent this morning, I am glad of it, because your urgency, I trust, arises from the possession of spiritual life. When you cannot live longer without

a Saviour, the Saviour will come to you, and you shall rejoice in Him.

Brethren, members of this church, as I have said on
another point, the same truth holds good with you. God
will come to bless you, and come speedily, when your
sense of need becomes deep and urgent. Oh, how great is
this church's need! We shall grow cold, unholy and worldly; there will be no conversions, there will be no additions
to our numbers; there will be diminutions, there will be
divisions, there will be mischief of all kinds; Satan will rejoice, and Christ will be dishonoured, unless we obtain a
larger measure of the Holy Spirit. Our need is urgent, and
when we feel that need thoroughly, then we shall get the
blessing which we want. Does any melancholy spirit say,
"We are in so bad a state that we cannot expect a large
blessing"? I reply, perhaps if we were worse, we should
obtain it all the sooner. I do not mean if we were really
so, but if we felt we were worse, we should be nearer the
blessing. When we mourn that we are in an ill state, then
we cry the more vehemently to God, and the blessing
comes. God never refused to go with Gideon because he
had not enough valiant men with him; but he paused because the people were too many. He brought them down
from thousands to hundreds, and he diminished the hundreds before he gave them victory. When you feel that you
must have God's presence, but that you do not deserve it,
and when your consciousness of this lays you in the dust,
then shall the blessing be vouchsafed.

For my part, brethren and sisters, I desire to feel a
spirit of urgency within my soul as I plead with God for
the dew of His grace to descend upon this church. I am not
bashful in this matter, for I have a license to pray. Mendi-
cancy[10] is forbidden in the streets, but, before the Lord I
am a licensed beggar. Jesus has said, "men ought always
to pray and not to faint." You land on the shores of a for-
eign country with the greatest confidence when you carry
a passport with you, and God has issued passports to His
children, by which they come boldly to His mercy seat; He
has invited you, He has encouraged you, He has bidden
you come to Him, and He has promised that whatsoever
ye ask in prayer, believing, ye shall receive. Come, then,
come urgently, come importunately, come with this plea,
"I am poor and needy; make no tarrying, O my God," and
a blessing shall surely come; it will not tarry. God grant we

10 Begging.

may see it, and give Him the glory of it.

IV. I am sorry to have been so brief where I had need to have enlarged, but I must close with the fourth point. Here is another part of the art and mystery of prayer—the soul grasping God. She has pleaded, and she has been urgent, but now she comes to close quarters; she grasps the covenant angel with one hand, "Thou art my help," and with the other, "Thou art my deliverer." Oh, those blessed "my's," those blessed potent "my's." The sweetness of the Bible lies in the possessive pronouns, and he who is taught to use them as the psalmist did, shall come off a conqueror with the eternal God. Now sinner, I pray God thou mayest be helped to say this morning to the blessed Christ of God, "Thou art my help and my deliverer." Perhaps you mourn that you cannot get that length, but, poor soul, hast thou any other help? If thou hast, then thou canst not hold two helpers with the same hand. "Oh, no," say you, "I have no help anywhere. I have no hope except in Christ." Well, then, poor soul, since thy hand is empty, that empty hand was made on purpose to grasp thy Lord with: lay hold on Him! Say to Him, this day, "Lord, I will hang on thee as poor lame Jacob did; now I cannot help myself, I will cleave to Thee: I will not let Thee go except Thou bless me." "Ah, it would be too bold," says one. But the Lord loves holy boldness in poor sinners; He would have you be bolder than you think of being. It is an unhallowed bashfulness that dares not trust a crucified Saviour. He died on purpose to save such as thou art; let Him have His way with thee, and do thou trust Him. "Oh," saith one, "but I am so unworthy." He came to seek and save the unworthy. He is not the Saviour of the self-righteous: He is the sinners' Saviour—"friend of sinners" is His name. Unworthy one, lay hold on Him! "Oh," saith one, "but I have no right." Well, since you have no right, your need shall be your claim: it is all the claim you want. Methinks I hear one say, "It is too late for me to plead for grace." It cannot be: it is impossible. While you live and desire mercy, it is not too late to seek it. Notice the parable of the man who wanted three loaves. I will tell you what crossed my mind when I read it: the man went to his friend at midnight; it could not have been later; for if he had been a little later than midnight, it would have been early in the morning, and so not late at all. It was midnight, and it could not be later; and so, if it is downright midnight with your soul, yet, be of good cheer, Jesus is an out of season Saviour; many of

His servants are "born out of due time." Any season is the right season to call upon the name of Jesus; therefore, only do not let the devil tempt thee with the thought that it can be too late. Go to Jesus now, go at once, and lay hold on the horns of the altar by the venturesome faith, and say, "Sacrifice for sinners, Thou art a sacrifice for me. Intercessor for the graceless, Thou art an intercessor for me. Thou Who distributest gifts to the rebellious, distribute gifts to me, for a rebel I have been." When we were yet without strength, in due time Christ died for the ungodly. "Such am I, Master; let the power of Thy death be seen in me to save my soul."

Oh, you that are saved and, therefore love Christ, I want you, dear brethren, as the saints of God, to practice this last part of my subject; and be sure to lay hold upon God in prayer. "Thou art my help and my deliverer." As a church we throw ourselves upon the strength of God, and we can do nothing without Him; but we do not mean to be without Him, we will hold Him fast. "Thou art my help and my deliverer." There was a boy at Athens, according to the old story, who used to boast that he ruled all Athens, and when they asked him how, he said, "Why, I rule my mother, my mother rules my father, and my father rules the city." He who knows how to be master of prayer will rule the heart of Christ, and Christ can and will do all things for His people, for the Father hath committed all things into His hands. You can be omnipotent if you know how to pray, omnipotent in all things which glorify God. What does the Word itself say? "Let him lay hold of my strength." Prayer moves the arm that moves the world. Oh for grace to grasp Almighty love in this fashion. We want more holdfast prayer; more tugging, and gripping, and wrestling, that saith, "I will not let thee go." That picture of Jacob at Jabbok shall suffice for us to close with. The covenant angel is there, and Jacob wants a blessing from him: he seems to put him off, but no put-offs will do for Jacob. Then the angel endeavours to escape from him, and tugs and strives; so he may, but no efforts shall make Jacob relax his grasp. At last the angel falls from ordinary wrestling to wounding him in the very seat of his strength; and Jacob will let his thigh go, and all his limbs go, but he will not let the angel go. The poor man's strength shrivels under the withering touch, but in his weakness he is still strong: he throws his arms about the mysterious man, and holds him as in a death-grip. Then the other says, "Let me go, for the day breaketh." Mark, he did not shake him off, he only said, "Let me go"; the angel will do nothing to force him to relax his hold, he leaves that to his voluntary will. The valiant Jacob cries, "No, I am set on it, I am resolved to win an answer to my prayer. I will not let thee go except thou bless me." Now, when the church begins to pray, it may be, at first, the Lord will make as though he would have gone further,[11] and we may fear that no answer will be given. Hold on, dear brethren. Be ye steadfast, unmovable, notwithstanding all. By-and-by, it may be, there will come discouragements where we looked for a flowing success; we shall find brethren hindering, some will be slumbering, and others sinning; backsliders and impenitent souls will abound; but let us not be turned aside. Let us be all the more eager. And if it should so happen that we ourselves become distressed and dispirited, and feel we never were so weak as we are now; never mind, brethren, still hold on, for when the sinew is shrunk the victory is near. Grasp with a tighter clutch than ever. Be this our resolution, "I will not let thee go except thou bless me." Remember the longer the blessing is coming the richer it will be when it arrives. That which is gained speedily by a single prayer is sometimes only a second rate blessing; but that which is gained after many a desperate tug, and many an awful struggle, is a full weighted and precious blessing. The children of importunity are always fair to look upon. The blessing which costs us the most prayer will be worth the most. Only let us be persevering in supplication, and we shall gain a broad far-reaching benediction for ourselves, the churches, and the world. I wish it were in my power to stir you all to fervent prayer; but I must leave it with the great author of all true supplication, namely, the Holy Spirit. May He work in us mightily, for Jesus' sake. Amen.

---

11 Luke 24:28

V. THE THRONE OF GRACE

The throne of grace.
Hebrews 4:16

These words are found embedded in that gracious verse, "Let us therefore come boldly unto the throne of grace, that we may obtain mercy, and find grace to help in time of need"; they are a gem in a golden setting. True prayer is an approach of the soul by the Spirit of God to the throne of God. It is not the utterance of words, it is not alone the feeling of desires, but it is the advance of the desires to God, the spiritual approach of our nature towards the Lord our God. True prayer is not a mere mental exercise, nor a vocal performance, but it is deeper far than that—it is spiritual commerce with the Creator of heaven and earth. God is a Spirit unseen of mortal eye, and only to be perceived by the inner man; our spirit within us, begotten by the Holy Ghost at our regeneration, discerns the Great Spirit, communes with him, prefers to him its requests, and receives from him answers of peace. It is a spiritual business from beginning to end; and its aim and object end not with man, but reach to God himself.

In order to such prayer, the work of the Holy Ghost himself is needed. If prayer were of the lips alone, we should only need breath in our nostrils to pray: if prayer were of the desires alone, many excellent desires are easily felt, even by natural men: but when it is the spiritual desire, and the spiritual fellowship of the human spirit with the Great Spirit, then the Holy Ghost himself must be present all through it, to help infirmity, and give life and power, or else true prayer will never be presented, but the thing offered to God will wear the name and have the form, but the inner life of prayer will be far from it.

Moreover, it is clear from the connection of our text, that the interposition of the Lord Jesus Christ is essential to acceptable prayer. As prayer will not be truly prayer without the Spirit of God, so it will not be prevailing prayer without the Son of God. He, the Great High Priest, must

go within the veil for us; nay, through his crucified person
the veil must be entirely taken away; for, until then, we
are shut out from the living God. The man who, despite
the teaching of Scripture, tries to pray without a Saviour
insults the Deity; and he who imagines that his own natural desires, coming up before God, unsprinkled with the
precious blood, will be an acceptable sacrifice before God,
makes a mistake; he has not brought an offering that God
can accept, any more than if he had struck off a dog's neck,
or offered an unclean sacrifice. Wrought in us by the Spirit, presented for us by the Christ of God, prayer becomes
power before the Most High, but not else.

In order, dear friends, that I may stir you up to prayer
this morning, and that your souls may be led to come near
to the Throne of Grace, I purpose to take these few words
and handle them as God shall give me ability. You have
begun to pray; God has begun to answer. This week has
been a very memorable one in the history of this church.
Larger numbers than ever before at one time have come
forward to confess Christ,—as plain an answer to the supplications of God's people, as though the hand of the Most
High had been stretched out of heaven handing down to
us the blessings for which we asked. Now, let us continue
in prayer, yea, let us gather strength in intercession, and
the more we succeed, the more earnest let us be to succeed yet more and more. Let us not be straitened in our
own bowels, since we are not straitened in our God. This
is a good day, and a time of glad tidings, and seeing that
we have the King's ear, I am most anxious that we should
speak to him for thousands of others; that they also, in answer to our pleadings, may be brought nigh unto Christ.

In trying to speak of the text this morning, I shall take
it thus: First, here is a throne; then, secondly, here is grace;
then we will put the two together, and we shall see grace
on a throne; and putting them together in another order,
we shall see sovereignty manifesting itself, and resplendent in grace.

II. Our text speaks of *a throne*:—"The Throne of
Grace." God is to be viewed in prayer as our Father; that
is the aspect which is dearest to us; but still we are not
to regard him as though he were such as we are; for our
Saviour has qualified the expression "Our Father," with
the words "who art in heaven"; and close at the heels of
that condescending name, in order to remind us that our
Father is still infinitely greater than ourselves, he has bid-

den us say, "Hallowed be thy name; thy kingdom come";
so that our Father is still to be regarded as a King, and in
prayer we come, not only to our Father's feet, but we come
also to the throne of the Great Monarch of the universe.
The mercy-seat is a throne, and we must not forget this.

If prayer should always be regarded by us as an en-
trance into the courts of the royalty of heaven; if we are
to behave ourselves as courtiers should in the presence of
an illustrious majesty, then we are not at a loss to know
the right spirit in which to pray. If in prayer we come to a
throne, it is clear that our spirit should, in the first place,
be one of lowly reverence. It is expected that the subject
in approaching to the king should pay him homage and
honour. The pride that will not own the king, the treason which rebels against the sovereign will should, if it
be wise, avoid any near approach to the throne. Let pride
bite the curb at a distance, let treason lurk in corners, for
only lowly reverence may come before the king himself
when he sits clothed in his robes of majesty. In our case,
the king before whom we come is the highest of all mon-
archs, the King of kings, the Lord of lords. Emperors are
but the shadows of his imperial power. They call themselves kings by right divine, but what divine right have
they? Common sense laughs their pretensions to scorn.
The Lord alone hath divine right, and to him only doth
the kingdom belong. He is the blessed and only potentate.
They are but nominal kings, to be set up and put down at
the will of men, or the decree of providence, but he is Lord
alone, the Prince of the kings of the earth.

> "He sits on no precarious throne,
>   Nor borrows leave to be."

My heart, be sure that thou prostrate thyself in such
a presence. If he be so great, place thy mouth in the dust
before him, for he is the most powerful of all kings; his
throne hath sway in all worlds; heaven obeys him cheerfully, hell trembles at his frown, and earth is constrained
to yield to him homage willingly or unwillingly. His power can make or can destroy. To create or to crush, either is
easy enough to him. My soul be thou sure that when thou
drawest nigh to the Omnipotent, who is as a consuming
fire, thou put thy shoes from off thy feet, and worship him
with lowliest humility.

Besides, he is the most Holy of all kings. His throne
is a great white throne, unspotted, and clear as crystal.

"The heavens are not pure in his sight, and he charged his angels with folly." And thou, a sinful creature, with what lowliness shouldst thou draw nigh to him. Familiarity there may be, but let it not be unhallowed. Boldness there should be, but let it not be impertinent. Still thou art on earth and he in heaven; still thou art a worm of the dust, a creature crushed before the moth, and he the Everlasting: before the mountains were brought forth, he was God, and if all created things should pass away again, yet still were he the same. My brethren, I am afraid we do not bow as we should before the Eternal Majesty; but, henceforth, let us ask the Spirit of God to put us in a right frame, that every one of our prayers may be a reverential approach to the Infinite Majesty above.

A throne, and therefore, in the second place, to be approached with devout joyfulness. If I find myself favoured by divine grace to stand amongst those favoured ones who frequent his courts, shall I not feel glad? I might have been in his prison, but I am before his throne: I might have been driven from his presence for ever, but I am permitted to come near to him, even into his royal palace, into his secret chamber of gracious audience, shall I not then be thankful? Shall not my thankfulness ascend into joy, and shall I not feel that I am honoured, that I am made the recipient of great favours when I am permitted to pray? Wherefore is thy countenance sad, O suppliant, when thou standest before the throne of grace? If thou wert before the throne of justice to be condemned for thine iniquities, thy hands might well be on thy loins; but now thou art favoured to come before the King in his silken robes of love, let thy face shine with sacred delight. If thy sorrows be heavy, tell them unto him, for he can assuage them; if thy sins be multiplied, confess them, for he can forgive them. O ye courtiers in the halls of such a monarch, be ye exceeding glad, and mingle praises with your prayers.

It is a throne, and therefore, in the third place, whenever it is approached, it should be with complete submission. We do not pray to God to instruct him as to what he ought to do, neither for a moment must we presume to dictate the line of the divine procedure. We are permitted to say unto God, "Thus and thus would we have it," but we must evermore add, "But, seeing that we are ignorant and may be mistaken—seeing that we are still in the flesh, and, therefore, may be actuated by carnal motives—not as we will, but as thou wilt." Who shall dictate to the throne?

No loyal child of God will for a moment imagine that he is to occupy the place of the King, but he bows before him who has a right to be Lord of all; and though he utters his desire earnestly, vehemently, importunately, and pleads and pleads again, yet it is evermore with this needful reservation: "Thy will be done, my Lord: and, if I ask anything that is not in accordance therewith, my inmost will is that thou wouldst be good enough to deny thy servant; I will take it as a true answer if thou refuse me, if I ask that which seemeth not good in thy sight." If we constantly remembered this, I think we should be less inclined to push certain suits before the throne, for we should feel, "I am here in seeking my own ease, my own comfort, my own advantage, and peradventure, I may be asking for that which would dishonour God; therefore will I speak with the deepest submission to the divine decrees."

But, brethren, in the fourth place, if it be a throne, it ought to be approached with enlarged expectations. Well doth our hymn put it:

> "Thou art coming to a king:
> Large petitions with thee bring."

We do not come, as it were, in prayer, only to God's almonry[12] where he dispenses his favours to the poor, nor do we come to the back-door of the house of mercy to receive the broken scraps, though that were more than we deserve; to eat the crumbs that fall from the Master's table is more than we could claim; but, when we pray, we are standing in the palace, on the glittering floor of the great King's own reception room, and thus we are placed upon a vantage ground. In prayer we stand where angels bow with veiled faces; there, even there, the cherubim and seraphim adore, before that selfsame throne to which our prayers ascend. And shall we come there with stunted requests, and narrow and contracted faith? Nay, it becomes not a King to be giving away pence[13] and groats,[14] he distributes pieces of broad gold; he scatters not as poor men must, scraps of bread and broken meat, but he makes a feast of fat things, of fat things full of marrow, of wines on

---

12 A place where alms were formerly distributed.

13 Pennies.

14 Hulled or crushed grain.

the lees[15] well refined. When Alexander's soldier was told to ask what he would, he did not ask stintedly after the nature of his own merits, but he made such a heavy demand, that the royal treasurer refused to pay it, and put the case to Alexander, and Alexander in right kingly sort replied: "He knows how great Alexander is, and he has asked as from a king; let him have what he requests." Take heed of imagining that God's thoughts are as thy thoughts, and his ways as thy ways. Do not bring before God stinted petitions and narrow desires, and say, "Lord, do according to these," but, remember, as high as the heavens are above the earth, so high are his ways above your ways, and his thoughts above your thoughts, and ask, therefore, after a God-like sort, ask for great things, for you are before the throne of grace, for then he would do for us exceeding abundantly above what we ask or even think.

And, beloved, I may add, in the fifth place, that the right spirit in which to approach the throne of grace, is that of unstaggering confidence. Who shall doubt the King? Who dares impugn the Imperial word? It was well said that if integrity were banished from the hearts of all mankind besides, it ought still to dwell in the hearts of kings. Shame on a king if he can lie. The veriest beggar in the streets is dishonoured by a broken promise, but what shall we say of a king if his word cannot be depended upon? Oh, shame upon us, if we are unbelieving before the throne of the King of heaven and earth. With our God before us in all his glory, sitting on the throne of grace, will our hearts dare to say we mistrust him? Shall we imagine either that he cannot, or will not, keep his promise? Banished be such blasphemous thoughts, and if they must come, let them come upon us when we are somewhere in the outskirts of his dominions, if such a place there be, but not in prayer, when we are in his immediate presence, and behold him in all the glory of his throne of grace. There, surely, is the place for the child to trust its Father, for the loyal subject to trust his monarch; and, therefore, far from it be all wavering or suspicion. Unstaggering faith should be predominant before the mercy-seat.

Only one other remark upon this point, and that is, that if prayer be a coming before the throne of God, it ought always to be conducted with the deepest sincerity, and in the spirit which makes everything real. If you are disloyal enough to despise the King, at least, for your own sake, do

---

15 The sediment of wine in the barrel.

not mock him to his face, and when he is upon his throne. If anywhere you dare repeat holy words without heart, let it not be in Jehovah's palace. If a person should ask for audience with royalty, and then should say, "I scarce know why I have come, I do not know that I have anything very particular to ask; I have no very urgent suit to press;" would he not be guilty both of folly and baseness? As for our great King, when we venture into his presence, let us have an errand there. As I said the other Sabbath, let us beware of playing at praying. It is insolence toward God. If I am called upon to pray in public, I must not dare to use words that are intended to please the ears of my fellow-worshippers, but I must realize that I am speaking to God himself, and that I have business to transact with the great Lord. And, in my private prayer, if, when I rise from my bed in the morning, I bow my knee and repeat certain words, or when I retire to rest at night go through the same regular form, I rather sin than do anything that is good, unless my very soul doth speak unto the Most High. Dost thou think that the King of heaven is delighted to hear thee pronounce words with a frivolous tongue, and a thoughtless mind? Thou knowest him not. He is a Spirit, and they that worship him must worship him in spirit and in truth. If thou hast any empty forms to prate,[16] go and pour them out into the ears of fools like thyself, but not before the Lord of Hosts. If thou hast certain words to utter, to which thou dost attach a superstitious reverence, go and say them in the bedizened[17] courts of the harlot Rome, but not before the glorious Lord of Zion. The spiritual God seeks spiritual worshipers, and such he will accept, and only such; but the sacrifice of the wicked is an abomination unto the Lord, and only a sincere prayer is his delight.

Beloved, the gathering up of all our remarks is just this,—prayer is no trifle. It is an eminent and elevated act. It is a high and wondrous privilege. Under the old Persian Empire a few of the nobility were permitted at any time to come in unto the king, and this was thought to be the highest privilege possessed by mortals. You and I, the people of God, have a permit, a passport to come before the throne of heaven at any time we will, and we are encouraged to come there with great boldness; but still let us not forget that it is no mean thing to be a courtier in the

---

16   To talk foolishly or tediously.

17   Gaudily decorated.

courts of heaven and earth, to worship him who made us and sustains us in being. Truly, when we attempt to pray, we may hear the voice saying out of the excellent glory: "Bow the knee." From all the spirits that behold the face of our Father who is in heaven, even now, I hear a voice which saith, "Oh, come let us worship and bow down, let us kneel before the Lord our Maker; for he is our God, and we are the people of his pasture and the sheep of his hand. O worship the Lord in the beauty of holiness; fear before him all the earth."

II. Lest the glow and brilliance of the word "throne" should be too much for mortal vision, our text now presents us with the soft, gentle radiance of that delightful word—"grace." We are called to the throne of grace, not to the throne of law. Rocky Sinai once was the throne of law, when God came to Paran with ten thousand of his holy ones. Who desired to draw near to that throne? Even Israel might not. Bounds were set about the mount, and if but a beast touched the mount, it was stoned or thrust through with a dart. O ye self-righteous ones who hope that you can obey the law, and think that you can be saved by it, look to the flames that Moses saw, and shrink, and tremble, and despair. To that throne we do not come now, for through Jesus the case is changed. To a conscience purged by the precious blood there is no anger upon the divine throne, though to our troubled minds—

"Once 'twas a seat of burning wrath,
 And shot devouring flame;
 Our God appeared consuming fire,
 And *jealous* was his name."

And, blessed be God, we are not this morning to speak of the throne of ultimate justice. Before that we shall all come, and as many of us as have believed will find it to be a throne of grace as well as of justice; for, he who sits upon that throne shall pronounce no sentence of condemnation against the man who is justified by faith. But I have not to call you this morning to the place from whence the resurrection-trumpet shall ring out so shrill and clear. Nor yet do we see the angels with their vengeful swords come forth to smite the foes of God; not yet are the great doors of the pit opened to swallow up the enemies who would not have the Son of God to reign over them. We are still on praying ground and pleading terms with God, and the throne to which we are bidden to come, and of which we

speak at this time, is the throne of grace. It is a throne set
up on purpose for the dispensation of grace; a throne from
which every utterance is an utterance of grace; the scepter
that is stretched out from it is the silver sceptre of grace;
the decrees proclaimed from it are purposes of grace; the
gifts that are scattered down its golden steps are gifts of
grace; and he that sits upon the throne is grace itself. It is
the throne of grace to which we approach when we pray;
and let us for a moment or two think this over, by way of
consolatory encouragement to those who are beginning to
pray; indeed, to all of us who are praying men and women.

If in prayer I come before a throne of grace, then the
faults of my prayer will be overlooked. In beginning to
pray, dear friends, you feel as if you did not pray. The
groanings of your spirit, when you rise from your knees
are such that you think there is nothing in them. What a
blotted, blurred, smeared prayer it is. Never mind; you
are not come to the throne of justice, else when God perceived the fault in the prayer he would spurn it,—your
broken words, your gaspings, and stammerings are before a throne of grace. When any one of us has presented his best prayer before God, if he saw it as God sees it,
there is no doubt he would make great lamentation over
it; for there is enough sin in the best prayer that was ever
prayed to secure its being cast away from God. But it is
not a throne of justice I say again, and here is the hope for
our lame, limping supplications. Our condescending King
does not maintain a stately etiquette in his court like that
which has been observed by princes among men, where
a little mistake or a flaw would secure the petitioner's being dismissed with disgrace. Oh, no; the faulty cries of his
children are not severely criticized by him. The Lord High
Chamberlain of the palace above, our Lord Jesus Christ,
takes care to alter and amend every prayer before he presents it, and he makes the prayer perfect with his perfec-
tion, and prevalent with His own merits. God looks upon
the prayer, as presented through Christ, and forgives all
its own inherent faultiness. How this ought to encourage
any of us who feel ourselves to be feeble, wandering, and
unskillful in prayer. If you cannot plead with God as sometimes you did in years gone by, if you feel as if somehow
or other you had grown rusty in the work of supplication,
never give over, but come still, yea and come oftener, for
it is not a throne of severe criticism, it is a throne of grace
to which you come.

Then, further, inasmuch as it is a throne of grace, the faults of the petitioner himself shall not prevent the success of his prayer. Oh, what faults there are in us! To come before a throne how unfit we are—we, that are all defiled with sin within and without! Dare any of you think of praying were it not that God's throne is a throne of grace? If you could, I confess that I could not. An absolute God, infinitely holy and just, could not in consistency with his divine nature answer any prayer from such a sinner as I am, were it not that he has arranged a plan by which my prayer comes up no longer to a throne of absolute justice, but to a throne which is also the mercy-seat, the propitiation, the place where God meets sinners, through Jesus Christ. Ah, I could not say to you, "Pray," not even to you saints, unless it were a throne of grace, much less could I talk of prayer to you sinners; but now I will say this to every sinner here, though he should think himself to be the worst sinner that ever lived, cry unto the Lord and seek him while he may be found. A throne of grace is a place fitted for you: go to your knees; by simple faith go to your Saviour, for he, he it is who is the throne of grace. It is in him that God is able to dispense grace unto the most guilty of mankind. Blessed be God, neither the faults of the prayer nor yet of the suppliant shall shut out our petitions from the God who delights in broken and contrite hearts.

If it be a throne of grace, then the desires of the pleader will be interpreted. If I cannot find words in which to utter my desires, God in his grace will read my desires without the words. He takes the meaning of his saints, the meaning of their groans. A throne that was not gracious would not trouble itself to make out our petitions; but God, the infinitely gracious One, will dive into the soul of our desires, and he will read there what we cannot speak with the tongue. Have you never seen the parent, when his child is trying to say something to him, and he knows very well what it is the little one has got to say, help him over the words and utter the syllables for him, and if the little one has half-forgotten what he would say, you have seen the father suggest the word: and so the ever-blessed Spirit, from the throne of grace, will help us and teach us words, nay, write in our hearts the desires themselves. We have in Scripture instances where God puts words into sinners' mouths. "Take with you words," saith he, "and say unto him, Receive us graciously and love us freely." He will put the desires, and put the expression of those desires into

your spirit by his grace; he will direct your desires to the
things which you ought to seek for; he will teach you your
wants, though as yet you know them not; he will suggest
to you his promises that you may be able to plead them;
he will, in fact, be Alpha and Omega to your prayer, just as
he is to your salvation; for as salvation is from first to last
of grace, so the sinner's approach to the throne of grace
is of grace from first to last. What comfort is this. Will we
not, my dear friends, with the greater boldness draw near
to this throne, as we suck out the sweet meaning of this
precious word, "the throne of grace"?

If it be a throne of grace, then all the wants of those
who come to it will be supplied. The King from off such
a throne will not say, "Thou must bring to Me gifts, thou
must offer to Me sacrifices." It is not a throne for receiving tribute; it is a throne for dispensing gifts. Come, then,
ye who are poor as poverty itself; come ye that have no
merits and are destitute of virtues, come ye that are re-
duced to a beggarly bankruptcy by Adam's fall and by
your own transgressions; this is not the throne of majesty
which supports itself by the taxation of its subjects, but a
throne which glorifies itself by streaming forth like a foun-
tain with floods of good things. Come ye, now, and receive
the wine and milk which are freely given, yea, come buy
wine and milk without money and without price. All the
petitioner's wants shall be supplied, because it is a throne
of grace.

And so, all the petitioner's miseries shall be compas-
sionated. Suppose I come to the throne of grace with the
burden of my sins; there is one on the throne who felt the
burden of sin in ages long gone by, and has not forgotten
its weight. Suppose I come loaded with sorrow; there is
One there who knows all the sorrows to which humanity
can be subjected. Am I depressed and distressed? Do I fear
that God himself has forsaken me? There is One upon the
throne who said, "My God, my God, why hast thou forsaken me?" It is a throne from which grace delights to look
upon the miseries of mankind with tender eye, to consider
them and to relieve them. Come, then; come, then; come,
then, ye that are not only poor, but wretched, whose miseries make you long for death, and yet dread it. Ye cap-
tive ones, come in your chains; ye slaves, come with the
irons upon your souls; ye who sit in darkness, come forth
all blindfold as you are. The throne of grace will look on
you if you cannot look on it, and will give to you, though

you have nothing to give in return, and will deliver you, though you cannot raise a finger to deliver yourself.

"The throne of grace." The word grows as I turn it over in my mind, and to me it is a most delightful reflection that if I come to the throne of God in prayer, I may feel a thousand defects, but yet there is hope. I usually feel more dissatisfied with my prayers than with anything else I do. I do not believe that it is an easy thing to pray in public so as to conduct the devotions of a large congregation aright. We sometimes hear persons commended for preaching well, but if any shall be enabled to pray well, there will be an equal gift and a higher grace in it. But, brethren, suppose in our prayers there should be defects of knowledge: it is a throne of grace, and our Father knoweth that we have need of these things. Suppose there should be defects of faith: he sees our little faith and still doth not reject it, small as it is. He doth not in every case measure out his gifts by the degree of our faith, but by the sincerity and trueness of faith. And if there should be grave defects in our spirit even, and failures in the fervency or in the humility of the prayer, still, though these should not be there and are much to be deplored; grace overlooks all this, forgives all this, and still its merciful hand is stretched out to enrich us according to our needs. Surely this ought to induce many to pray who have not prayed, and should make us who have been long accustomed to use the consecrated art of prayer, to draw near with greater boldness than ever to the throne of grace.

III. But, now regarding our text as a whole, it conveys to us the idea of grace enthroned. It is a throne, and who sits on it? It is grace personified that is here installed in dignity. And, truly, today grace is on a throne. In the gospel of Jesus Christ grace is the most predominant attribute of God. How comes it to be so exalted? We reply, well, grace has a throne by conquest. Grace came down to earth in the form of the Well-beloved, and it met with sin. Long and sharp was the struggle, and grace appeared to be trampled under foot of sin; but grace at last seized sin, threw it on its own shoulders, and, though all but crushed beneath the burden, grace carried sin up to the cross and nailed it there, slew it there, put it to death for ever, and triumphed gloriously. For this cause at this hour grace sits on a throne, because it has conquered human sin, has borne the penalty of human guilt, and overthrown all its enemies.

Grace, moreover, sits on the throne because it has established itself there by right. There is no injustice in the grace of God. God is as just when he forgives a believer as when he casts a sinner into hell. I believe in my own soul that there is as much and as pure a justice in the acceptance of a soul that believes in Christ as there will be in the rejection of those souls who die impenitent, and are banished from Jehovah's presence. The sacrifice of Christ has enabled God to be just, and yet the justifier of him that believeth. He who knows the word "substitution," and can spell its meaning aright, will see that there is nothing due to punitive justice from any believer, seeing that Jesus Christ has paid all the believer's debts, and now God would be unjust if he did not save those for whom Christ vicariously suffered, for whom his righteousness was provided, and to whom it is imputed. Grace is on the throne by conquest, and sits there by right.

Grace is enthroned this day, brethren, because Christ has finished his work and gone into the heavens. It is enthroned in power. When we speak of its throne, we mean that it has unlimited might. Grace sits not on the footstool of God; grace stands not in the courts of God, but it sits on the throne; it is the regnant[18] attribute; it is the king today. This is the dispensation of grace, the year of grace: grace reigns through righteousness unto eternal life. We live in the era of reigning grace, for seeing he ever liveth to make intercession for the sons of men, Jesus is able also to save them to the uttermost that come unto God by him. Sinner, if you were to meet grace in the by-way, like a traveller on his journey, I would bid you make its acquaintance and ask its influence; if you should meet grace as a merchant on the exchange, with treasure in his hand, I would bid you court its friendship, it will enrich you in the hour of poverty; if you should see grace as one of the peers of heaven, highly exalted, I would bid you seek to get its ear; but, oh, when grace sits on the throne, I beseech you close in with it at once. It can be no higher, it can be no greater, for it is written "God is love," which is an alias for grace. Oh, come and bow before it; come and adore the infinite mercy and grace of God. Doubt not, halt not, hesitate not. Grace is reigning; grace is God; God is love. Oh that you, seeing grace is thus enthroned, would come and receive it. I say, then, that grace is enthroned by conquest, by right, and by power, and, I will add, it is enthroned in glory, for

---

18 Reigning, ruling.

God glorifies his grace. It is one of his objects now to make his grace illustrious. He delights to pardon penitents, and so to show his pardoning grace; he delights to look upon wanderers and restore them, to show his reclaiming grace; he delights to look upon the broken-hearted and comfort them, that he may show his consoling grace. There is a grace to be had of various kinds, or rather the same grace acting different ways, and God delights to make his grace glorious. There is a rainbow round about the throne like unto an emerald, the emerald of his compassion and his love. O happy souls that can believe this, and believing it can come at once and glorify grace by becoming instances of its power.

IV. Lastly, our text, if rightly read, has in it sovereignty resplendent in glory,—the glory of grace. The mercy seat is a throne; though grace is there, it is still a throne. Grace does not displace sovereignty. Now, the attribute of sovereignty is very high and terrible; its light is like unto a jasper stone, most precious, and like unto a sapphire stone, or, as Ezekiel calls it, "the terrible crystal." Thus saith the King, the Lord of hosts: "I will have mercy on whom I will have mercy, and I will have compassion on whom I will have compassion." "Who art thou, O man, that repliest against God? Shall the thing formed say to him that formed it, Why hast thou made me thus?" "Hath not the potter power over the clay to make of the same lump one vessel unto honour and another unto dishonour?" These are great and terrible words, and are not to be answered. He is a King, and he will do as he wills. None shall stay his hand, or say unto him, What doest thou? But, ah! lest any of you should be downcast by the thought of his sovereignty, I invite you to the text. It is a throne,—there is sovereignty; but to every soul that knows how to pray, to every soul that by faith comes to Jesus, the true mercy seat, divine sovereignty wears no dark and terrible aspect, but is full of love. It is a throne of grace; from which I gather that the sovereignty of God to a believer, to a pleader, to one who comes to God in Christ, is always exercised in pure grace. To you, to you who come to God in prayer, the sovereignty always runs thus: "I will have mercy on that sinner; though he deserves it not, though in him there is no merit, yet because I can do as I will with my own, I will bless him, I will make him my child, I will accept him; he shall be mine in the day when I make up my jewels." On the mercy seat God never executed sovereignty otherwise than in a way of grace. He reigns, but in this case grace reigns through righteousness unto eternal life by Jesus Christ our Lord.

There are these two or three things to be thought of, and I have done. On the throne of grace sovereignty has placed itself under bonds of love. I must speak with words choice and picked here, and I must hesitate and pause to get the right sentences, lest I err while endeavouring to speak the truth in plainness. God will do as he wills; but, on the mercy seat, he is under bonds—bonds of his own making, for he has entered into covenant with Christ, and so into covenant with his chosen. Though God is and ever must be a sovereign, he never will break his covenant, not alter the word that is gone out of his mouth. He cannot be false to a covenant of his own making. When I come to God in Christ, to God on the mercy seat, I need not imagine that by any act of sovereignty God will set aside his covenant. That cannot be: it is impossible.

Moreover, on the throne of grace, God is again bound to us by his promises. The covenant contains in it many gracious promises, exceeding great and precious. "Ask and it shall be given you; seek and ye shall find; knock and it shall be opened unto you." Until God had said that word or a word to that effect, it was at his own option to hear prayer or not, but it is not so now; for now, if it be true prayer offered through Jesus Christ, his truth binds him to hear it. A man may be perfectly free, but the moment he makes a promise, he is not free to break it; and the everlasting God wants not to break his promise. He delights to fulfil it. He hath declared that all his promises are yea and amen in Christ Jesus; but, for our consolation when we survey God under the high and terrible aspect of a sovereign, we have this to reflect on, that he is under covenant bonds of promise to be faithful to the souls that seek him. His throne must be a throne of grace to his people.

And, once more, and sweetest thought of all, every covenant promise has been endorsed and sealed with blood, and far be it from the everlasting God to pour scorn upon the blood of his dear Son. When a king has given a charter to a city, he may before have been absolute, and there may have been nothing to check his prerogatives, but when the city has its charter, then it pleads its rights before the king. Even thus God has given to his people a charter of untold blessings, bestowing upon them the sure mercies of David. Very much of the validity of a charter

depends upon the signature and the seal, and, my brethren, how sure is the charter of covenant grace. The signature is the hand-writing of God himself, and the seal is the
blood of the Only-begotten. The covenant is ratified with
blood, the blood of his own dear Son. It is not possible that
we can plead in vain with God when we plead the blood-
sealed covenant, ordered in all things and sure. Heaven
and earth shall pass away, but the power of the blood of
Jesus with God can never fail. It speaks when we are silent,
and it prevails when we are defeated. Better things than
that of Abel doth it ask for, and its cry is heard. Let us
come boldly, for we hear the promise in our hearts. When
we feel alarmed because of the sovereignty of God, let us
cheerfully sing—

    "The gospel bears my spirit up,
     A faithful and unchanging God
     Lays the foundation for my hope
     In oaths, and promises, and blood."

May God the Holy Spirit help us to use aright from
this time forward "the throne of grace." Amen.

VI. Brief, Silent Prayer

So I prayed to the God of Heaven.
Nehemiah 2:4.

Nehemiah had made inquiry as to the state of the city of Jerusalem and the tidings he heard caused him bitter grief. "Why should not my countenance be sad," he said, "when the city, the place of my fathers' sepulchers, lies waste and the gates thereof are consumed with fire?" He could not endure that it should be a mere ruinous heap—that city which was once beautiful and the joy of the whole earth! Laying the matter to heart, he did not begin to speak to other people about what they would do, nor did he draw up a wonderful scheme about what might be done if so many thousand people joined in the enterprise.

No, it occurred to him that he should do something himself. This is just the way that practical men start a matter. The unpractical will plan, arrange and speculate about what may be done, but the genuine, thorough-going lover of Zion puts this question to himself—"What can you do? Nehemiah, what can you, yourself, do? Come, it has to be done, and you are the man that is to do it—at least, to do your share. What can you do?" Coming so far, he resolved to set apart a time for prayer. It never left his thoughts for nearly four months! Day and night Jerusalem seemed written on his heart, as if the name was painted on his eyeballs. He could only see Jerusalem. When he slept he dreamed about Jerusalem. When he woke, the first thought was, "Poor Jerusalem!", and before he fell asleep again his evening prayer was for the ruined walls of Jerusalem.

The man of one thing, you know, is a terrible man—and when one single passion has absorbed the whole of his manhood, something will be sure to come of it. Depend upon that. The desire of his heart will develop into some open demonstration, especially if he talks the matter over with God in prayer. Something did come of this. Before long Nehemiah had an opportunity. Men of God, if you want to serve God and cannot find the propitious[19] occasion, wait awhile in prayer and your opportunity will break on your path like a sunbeam! There was never a true and valiant heart that failed to find a fitting sphere somewhere or other in God's service. Every diligent laborer is needed in some part of His vineyard. You may have to linger. You may seem as if you stood in the market idle because your Master would not engage you, but wait there in prayer—and with your heart boiling over with a warm purpose—your chance will come.

The hour will need its man and if you are ready, you, as a man, shall not be without your hour. God sent Nehemiah an opportunity. That opportunity came, 'tis true, in a way which he could not have expected. It came through his own sadness of heart. This matter preyed upon his mind till he began to look exceedingly unhappy. I cannot tell whether others noticed it, but the king whom he served, when he went into court with the royal goblet, noticed the distress on the cupbearer's countenance and said to him, "Why is your countenance sad, seeing you are not sick? This is nothing else but sorrow of heart."

Nehemiah little knew that his prayer was making the occasion for him. The prayer was registering itself upon his face. His fasting was making its marks upon his visage and, though he did not know it, he was, in that way, preparing the opportunity for himself when he went in before the king. But you see, when the opportunity did come, there was trouble with it, for he says, "I was very sore afraid." You want to serve God, young man. You want to be at work. Perhaps you do not know what that work involves. It is not all pleasure. You are longing for the battle, young soldier—you have not smelled powder, yet, and when you have been in a battle and have had a few cuts, or a bullet or two have pierced you—you may not feel quite so eager for the fray!

Yet the courageous man sets those things aside and is ready to serve his country or his sovereign. And so the courageous Christian puts all difficulty aside and he is ready to serve his comrades and his God, cost what it may! What if I should be sore afraid? Yet so let it be, my God, if thus there shall be an opportunity to seek and to secure the welfare of Jerusalem for Your servant who longs to promote it with all his heart. Thus have we traced Nehemiah up to the particular point where our text concerns him.

---

19 Favorable.

The king, Artaxerxes, having asked him why he was sad, he had an opportunity of telling him that the city of his fathers was a ruin. Thereupon the king asks him what he really wishes. By the manner of the question he would seem to imply an assurance that he means to help Nehemiah.

And here we are somewhat surprised to find that instead of promptly answering the king—the answer is not given immediately—an incident occurs, a fact is related. Though he was a man who had lately given himself up to prayer and fasting, this little parenthesis occurs—"So I prayed to the God of Heaven." My preamble leads up to this parenthesis. Upon this prayer I propose to preach. The fact that Nehemiah prayed challenges attention! He had been asked a question by his sovereign. The proper thing, you would suppose, was to answer it. Not so. Before he answered, he prayed to the God of Heaven. I do not suppose the king noticed the pause. Probably the interval was not long enough to be noticed, but it was long enough for God to notice it—long enough for Nehemiah to have sought and have obtained guidance from God as to how to frame his answer to the king.

Are you not surprised to find a man of God having time to pray to God between a question and an answer? Yet Nehemiah found that time. We are the more astonished at his praying because he was so evidently perturbed in mind, for, according to the second verse, he was very afraid. When you are fluttered and put out, you may forget to pray. Do you not, some of you, account it a valid excuse for omitting your ordinary devotion? At least, if anyone had said to you, "You did not pray when you were about that business," you would have replied, "How could I? There was a question that I was obliged to answer. I dared not hesitate. It was a king that asked it. I was in a state of confusion. I really was so distressed and terrified that I was not master of my own emotions. I hardly knew what I did. If I did not pray, surely the omission may be overlooked. I was in a state of wild alarm."

Nehemiah, however, felt that if he was alarmed, it was a reason for praying, not for forgetting to pray! So habitually was he in communion with God, that as soon as he found himself in a dilemma, he flew away to God, just as the dove would fly to hide herself in the clefts of the rock. His prayer was the more remarkable on this occasion because he must have felt very eager about his objective. The king asks him what it is he needs and his whole heart is set

upon building up Jerusalem. Are you not surprised that he
did not at once say, "O king, live forever! I long to build
up Jerusalem's walls. Give me all the help you can"? But
no, eager as he was to pounce upon the desired objective,
he withdraws his hand until it is said, "So I prayed to the
God of Heaven."

I confess I admire him! I desire, also, to imitate him.
I would that every Christian's heart might have just that
holy caution that did not permit him to make such haste as
to find ill-speed. "Prayer and provender[20] hinder no man's
journey." Certainly, when the desire of our heart is close
before us, we are anxious to seize it. But we shall be all the
surer of getting the bird we spy in the bush to be a bird we
grasp in the hand if we quietly pause, lift up our heart and
pray the God of Heaven! It is all the more surprising that
he should have deliberately prayed just then because he
had been already praying for the past three or four months
concerning the same matter. Some of us would have said,
"That is the thing I have been praying for—now all I have
to do is to take it and use it! Why pray any more? After
all, my midnight tears and daily cries, and setting myself
apart by fasting to cry unto the God of Heaven—after
such an anxious conference, surely, at last, the answer has
come! What is to be done but to take the good that God
provides me and rejoice in it?"

But no, you will always find that the man who has
prayed much is the man who prays more. "For unto everyone that has, shall be given, and he shall have abundance."
If you do but know the sweet art of prayer, you are the
man that will be often engaged in it. If you are familiar
with the Mercy Seat, you will constantly visit it—

> "For who that knows the power of prayer
> But wishes to be often there?"

Although Nehemiah had been praying all this while,
he nevertheless must offer another petition. "So I prayed
to the God of Heaven." One thing more is worth remem-
bering, namely that he was in a king's palace and in the
palace of a heathen king, too—and he was in the very act
of handing up to the king a goblet of wine. He was fulfill-
ing his part in the state festival, I doubt not, among the
glare of lamps and the glitter of gold and silver. He was
in the midst of princes and peers of the realm. Or even

---

20 Food, nourishment.

if it were a private festival with the king and queen only,
yet still men generally feel so impressed on such occasions
with the responsibility of their high position that they are
apt to forget prayer.

But this devout Israelite, at such a time and in such
a place, when he stands at the king's foot to hold up to
him the golden goblet, refrains from answering the king's
question until first he has prayed to the God of Heav-
en! There are the facts and I think that seems to prompt
further inquiry. So we pass on to observe the manner of
this prayer. Well, very briefly, it was what we call a brief
prayer—prayer which, as it were, hurls a dart and then
it is done. It was not the prayer which stands knocking
at Mercy's door—knock, knock, knock—but it was the
concentration of many knocks into one. It was begun and
completed, as it were, with one stroke! This brief prayer I
desire to commend to you as among the very best forms
of prayer.

Notice how very short it must have been. It was in-
troduced—slipped in—sandwiched in between the king's
question and Nehemiah's answer. And, as I have already
said, I do not suppose it took up any time at all that was
appreciable—scarcely a second. Most likely the king never observed any kind of pause or hesitation, for Nehemiah was in such a state of alarm at the question that I am
persuaded he did not allow any demur or vacillation to
appear. The prayer must have been offered like an electric
flash, very rapidly, indeed! In certain states of strong excitement it is wonderful how much the mind gets through
in a short time. You may, perhaps, have dreamed and
your dream occupied, to your idea, an hour or two at the
very least. Yet it is probably—no, I think certain—that all
dreaming is done at the moment you awake. You never
dreamed at all when you were asleep—it was just in that
instant when you awoke that the whole of it went through
your mind.

As drowning men, when rescued and recovered, have
been heard to say that while they were sinking they say
the whole panorama of their lives pass before them in a
few seconds, so the mind must be capable of accomplish-
ing much in a brief space of time. Thus the prayer was
presented like the blinking of an eye—it was done intui-
tively, yet it was done—and it proved to be a prayer that
prevailed with God. We know, also, that it must have been
a silent prayer and not merely silent as to sounds but si-

lent as to any outward signs—perfectly secret. Artaxerxes never knew that Nehemiah prayed, though he stood,
probably, within a yard of him. He did not even move his
lips as Hannah did, nor did he deem it right, even, to close
his eyes. The prayer was strictly within himself offered to
God.

As in the innermost shrine of the Temple—in the Holy
of Holies of his own secret soul—there did he pray. Short
and silent was the prayer. It was a prayer on the spot. He
did not go to his chamber, as Daniel did, and open the
window. Daniel was right, but this was a different occasion. Nehemiah could not have been permitted to retire
from the palace just then. He did not even turn his face to
the wall or seek a corner of the apartment. No, but then
and there, with the cup in his hand, he prayed unto the
God of Heaven—and then answered the question of the
king. I have no doubt from the very wording of the text
that it was a very intense and direct prayer. He says, "So
I prayed to the God of Heaven." That was Nehemiah's fa-
vorite name of God—the God of Heaven.

He knew to whom he was praying. He did not draw
a bow at a venture and shoot his prayers anyway, but he
prayed to the God of Heaven—a right straight prayer to
God for the thing he needed—and his prayer sped, though
it occupied less, perhaps, than a second of time. It was a
prayer of a remarkable kind. I know it was so, because Nehemiah never forgot that he prayed it. I have prayed hundreds of times—thousands of times—and not remembered
any particulars, afterwards, either as to the occasion that
prompted or the emotions that excited me. But there are
one or two prayers in my life that I can never forget. I have
not jotted them down in a diary, but I remember when
I prayed, because the time was so special and the prayer
was so intense—and the answer to it was so remarkable!

Now, Nehemiah's prayer was never, never erased
from his memory. And when these words of history were
written down he wrote that down. "So I prayed to the God
of Heaven"—a little bit of a prayer pushed in edgeways
between a question and an answer—a mere fragment of
devotion, as it seemed, and yet so important that it is put
down in a historical document as a part of the history of
the restitution and rebuilding of the city of Jerusalem!
And it was a link in the circumstances which led up to that
event of the most important character. Nehemiah felt it to
be so and, therefore, he notes the record—"So I prayed to

the God of Heaven."

Now, beloved friends, I come, in the third place, to recommend to you this excellent style of praying. I shall speak mainly to the children of God—to you that have faith in God. I beg you often, no, I would ask you always to use this method of brief, silent prayer. And I would to God, also, that some here who have never prayed before would offer a brief, silent prayer to the God of Heaven before they leave this house—that a short but fervent petition, something like that of the publican in the temple, might go up from you—"God be merciful to me, a sinner."

To deal with this matter practically, then, it is the duty and privilege of every Christian to have set times of prayer. I cannot understand a man's keeping up the vitality of godliness unless he regularly retires for prayer, morning and evening at the very least. Daniel prayed three times a day and David says, "Seven times a day will I praise You." It is good for your hearts, good for your memory, good for your moral consistency that you should hedge about certain portions of time and say, "These belong to God. I shall do business with God at such-and-such a time and try to be as punctual to my hours with Him as I should be if I made an engagement to meet a friend."

When Sir Thomas Abney was Lord Mayor of London, the banquet somewhat troubled him, for Sir Thomas always had prayer with his family at a certain time. The difficulty was how to leave the banquet to keep up family devotion. But so important did he consider it that he vacated his chair, saying to a person near that he had a special engagement with a dear Friend which he must keep. And he did keep it and returned, again, to his place, none of the company being the wiser, but he himself being all the better for observing his habit of worship!

But now, having urged the importance of such habitual piety, I want to impress on you the value of another sort of prayer—namely, the short, brief, quick, frequent prayers of which Nehemiah gives us a specimen. And I recommend this because it hinders no engagement and occupies no time. You may be measuring off your calicoes, or weighing your groceries, or you may be casting up an account and between the items you may say, "Lord, help me." You may breathe a prayer to Heaven and say, "Lord, keep me." It will take no time. It is one great advantage to persons who are hard pressed in business that such prayers as these will not, in the slightest degree, incapacitate them from attending to the business they may have in hand!

It requires you to go to no particular place. You can stand where you are, ride in a cab, walk along the streets, be the bottom sawyer[21] in a saw pit, or the top one and yet pray just as well such prayers as these. No altar, no Church, no so-called sacred place is needed! Wherever you are, just a little prayer as that will reach the ear of God and win a blessing. Such a prayer as that can be offered anywhere, under any circumstances. I do not know in what condition a man could be in which he might not offer some such prayer as that. On the land, or on the sea, in sickness or in health, amidst losses or gains, great reverses or good returns, still might he breathe his soul in short, quick sentences to God! The advantage of such a way of praying is that you can pray often and pray always. If you must prolong your prayer for a quarter of an hour you might possibly be unable to spare the time, but if it only needs a quarter of a minute, why, then, it may come again and again and again and again—a hundred times a day!

The habit of prayer is blessed, but the spirit of prayer is better. And the spirit of prayer it is which is the mother of these brief, silent prayers and, therefore, do I like them because she is a plentiful mother. Many times in a day may we speak with the Lord our God. Such prayer may be suggested by all sorts of surroundings. I remember a poor man once paying me a compliment which I highly valued at the time. He was lying in a hospital and when I called to see him he said, "I heard you for some years, and now whatever I look at seems to remind me of something or other that you said, and it comes back to me as fresh as when I first heard it." Well, now, he that knows how to pray brief prayers will find everything about him helping him to the sacred habit! Is it a beautiful landscape? Say, "Blessed be God who has strewn these treasures of form and color through the world, to cheer the sight and gladden the heart."

Are you in doleful darkness and is it a foggy day? Say, "Lighten my darkness, O Lord." Are you in the midst of company? You will be reminded to pray, "Lord, keep the door of my lips." Are you quite alone? Then you can say, "Let me not be alone, but be You with me, Father." The putting on of your clothes, the sitting at the breakfast table, the getting into the conveyance, the walking the streets,

---

21 A person who saws timber for a living.

the opening of your ledger, the putting up of your shut-
ters—everything may suggest such prayer as that which
I am trying to describe if you are but in the right frame of
mind for offering it.

These prayers are commendable because they are truly spiritual. Wordy prayers may, also, be windy prayers!
There is much of praying by book that has nothing whatever to recommend it. Pray with your heart, not with your
hands. Or, if you would lift hands in prayer, let them be
your own hands, not another man's. The prayers that
come leaping out of the soul—the gust of strong emotion,
fervent desire, lively faith—these are the truly spiritual
prayers and no prayers but spiritual prayers will God accept. This kind of prayer is free from any suspicion that
it is prompted by the corrupt motive of being offered to
please men. They cannot say that the secret prayers of our
soul are presented with any view to our own praise, for no
man knows that we are praying at all! Therefore do I commend such prayers to you and hope that you may abound
in them.

There have been hypocrites that have prayed by the
hour. I doubt not there are hypocrites as regular at their
devotions as the angels are before the Throne of God—and
yet there is no life, no spirit, no acceptance in their pre-
tentious homage! But he that prays brief prayers—whose
heart talks with God—he is no hypocrite! There is a reality, force and life about his prayers. Brief, silent prayers
are of great use to us. Oftentimes they check us. Bad-tem-
pered people, if you were always to pray just a little before
you let angry expressions fly from your lips, why many
times you would not say those naughty words at all! They
advised a good woman to take a glass of water and hold
some of it in her mouth five minutes before she scolded
her husband. I dare say it was not a bad recipe, but if, instead of practicing that little eccentricity, she would just
breathe a short prayer to God it would certainly be more
effectual and far more Scriptural.

I can recommend it as a valuable prescription for the
hasty and the peevish—for all who are quick to take of-
fense and slow to forgive insult or injury. When in business
you are about to close in with an offer about the propriety
of which you have a little doubt, or a positive scruple, such
a prayer as, "Guide me, good Lord" would often keep you
back from doing what you will afterwards regret. The habit of offering these brief prayers would, also, check your

confidence in yourself. It would show your dependence upon God. It would keep you from getting worldly. It would be like sweet perfume burnt in the chamber of your soul to keep away the fever of the world from your heart.

Besides, this type of prayers actually bring us blessings from Heaven. Brief prayers, as in the case of Eliezer, the servant of Abraham. As in the case of Jacob when he said, even in dying, "I have waited for Your salvation, O God"—prayers such as Moses offered when we do not read that he prayed at all and yet God said to him, "Why cry you unto Me?" And brief prayers such as David frequently presented—these were all successful with the Most High. Therefore abound in them, for God loves to encourage and to answer them! I might thus keep on recommending brief prayer, but I will say only one more thing in its favor.

I believe it is very suitable to some persons of a peculiar temperament who could not pray for a long time to save their lives. Their minds are rapid and quick. Well, time is not an element in the business—God does not hear us because of the length of our prayer—but because of the sincerity of it. Prayer is not to be measured by the yard, nor weighed by the pound. It is the might and force of it—the truth and reality of it—the energy and the intensity of it. You that are either of so little a mind or of so quick a mind that you cannot use many words or continue long to think of one thing, it should be to your comfort that brief prayers are acceptable.

And it may be, dear friend, that you are in a condition of body in which you cannot pray any other way. A headache such as some people are frequently affected with the major part of their lives—a state of body which only the physician can explain to you—might prevent the mind from concentrating itself long upon one subject. Then it is refreshing to be able again and again and again—fifty or a hundred times a day—to address one's self to God in short, quick sentences, the soul being all on fire. This is a blessed style of praying!

Now, I conclude by mentioning a few of the times when I think we ought to resort to this practice of brief prayer. Mr. Rowland Hill was a remarkable man for the depth of his piety, but when I asked at Wotton-under-Edge for his study, though I rather pressed the question, I did not obtain a satisfactory reply. At length the good minister said, "The fact is, we never found any. Mr. Hill used to study in the garden, in the parlor, in the bedroom, in the streets, in the woods, anywhere." "But where did he retire for prayer?" They said they supposed it was in his chamber, but that he was always praying—that it did not matter where he was, the good old man was always praying! It seemed as if his whole life, though he spent it in the midst of his fellow men doing good, was passed in perpetual prayer!

You know the story of his being in Walworth, at Mr. George Clayton's chapel, and of his being seen in the aisles after everybody was gone, while he was waiting for his coachman. There was the old man toddling up and down the aisles, and as someone listened, he heard him singing to himself—

"And when I shall die, receive me I'll cry,
 For Jesus has loved me, I cannot tell why.
 But this thing I find, we two are so joined,
 He won't be in Heaven and leave me behind."

And with such rhymes and ditties, and choice words, he would occupy every moment of his life! He has been known to stand in the Blackfriars' road with his hands under his coat tails, looking in a shop window, and if you listened you might soon perceive that he was breathing out his soul before God! He had got into a constant state of prayer! I believe it is the best condition in which a man can be—praying always, praying without ceasing, always drawing near to God with these brief prayers.

But if I must give you a selection of suitable times I should mention such as these. Whenever you have a great joy, cry, "Lord, make this a real blessing to me." Do not exclaim with others, "Am I not a lucky fellow?" but say, "Lord, give me more grace and more gratitude, now that You do multiply Your favors." When you have got any arduous undertaking on hand or a heavy piece of business, do not touch it till you have breathed your soul out in a short prayer. When you have a difficulty before you and you are seriously perplexed. When business has got into a tangle or a confession which you cannot unravel or arrange, breathe a prayer! It need not occupy a minute, but it is wonderful how many snarls come loose after just a word of prayer.

Are the children particularly troublesome to you, good woman? Do you seem as if your patience was almost worn out with the worry and harassment? Now for a brief prayer! You will manage them all the better and you will bear with their naughty tempers all the more quietly. At any rate your own mind will be the less ruffled. Do you think that there is a temptation before you? Do you begin to suspect that somebody is plotting against you? Now for a prayer. "Lead me in a plain path because of my enemies." Are you at work at the bench, or in a shop, or a warehouse where lewd conversation and shameful blasphemies assail your ears? Now for a short prayer! Have you noticed some sin that grieves you? Let it move you to prayer! These things ought to remind you to pray.

I believe the devil would not let people swear so much if Christian people always prayed every time they heard an oath. He would then see it did not pay. Their blasphemies might somewhat be hushed if they provoked us to supplication! Do you feel your own heart going off the lines? Does sin begin to fascinate you? Now for a prayer—a warm, earnest, passionate cry, "Lord, hold me up!" Did you see something with your eyes and did that infect your heart? Do you feel as if "your feet were almost gone and your steps had well near slipped?" Now for a prayer—"Hold me, Lord, by my right hand." Has something quite unlooked-for happened? Has a friend treated you badly? Then, like David, say, "Lord, put to nothing the counsel of Ahithophel."

Breathe a prayer now! Are you anxious to do some good? Be sure to have prayer over it. Do you mean to speak to that young man about his soul? Pray first, brothers and sisters. Do you mean to address yourself to the members of your class and write them a letter this week about their spiritual welfare? Pray over every line, brothers and sisters. It is always good to have praying going on while you are talking about Christ! I always find I can preach better if I can pray while I am preaching. And the mind is very remarkable in its activities. It can be praying while it is studying—it can be looking up to God while it is talking to man! And there can be one hand held up to receive supplies from God while the other hand is dealing out the same supplies which He is pleased to give!

Pray as long as you live! Pray when you are in great pain—the sharper the pang—the more urgent and importunate should your cry to God be. And when the shadow of death gathers round you and strange feelings flush or chill you, and plainly tell that you near the journey's end, then pray! Oh that is a time for brief prayer! Short and

pithy prayers like this—"Hide not Your face from me, O
Lord." Or this, "Be not far from me, O God" will doubtless
suit you. "Lord Jesus, receive my spirit," were the thrilling
words of Stephen in his extremity! And "Father, into Your
hands I commend My spirit," were the words that your
Master, Himself, uttered just before He bowed His head
and gave up the ghost. You may well take up the same
strain and imitate Him.

These thoughts and counsels are so exclusively ad-
dressed to the saints and faithful brothers and sisters in
Christ that you will be prone to ask. "Is not there anything
to be said to the unconverted?" Well, whatever has been
spoken in their hearing may be used by them for their own
benefit. Now let me address myself to you as pointedly as
I can. Though you are not saved, yet you must not say, "I
cannot pray." Why, if prayer is so simple, what excuse can
you have for neglecting it? It needs no measurable space of
time. Such prayers as these, God will hear, and you have,
all of you, the ability and opportunity to think and to express them if you have only that elementary faith in God
which believes "that He is, and that He is a rewarder of
them that diligently seek Him."

Cornelius had, I suppose, got about as far as this when
he was admonished by the angel to send for Peter, who
preached to him peace by Jesus Christ to the conversion of
his soul! Is there such a strange being in the Tabernacle as a
man or woman that never prays? How shall I expostulate
with you? May I steal a passage from a living poet who,
though he has contributed nothing to our hymn books,
hums a note so suited to my purpose and so pleasant to
my ear that I like to quote it—

> "More things are worked by prayer
>   Than this world dreams of.
>   Therefore let your voice
>   Rise like a fountain, flowing night and day!
>   For what are men better than sheep or goats,
>   That nourish a blind life within the brain,
>   If, knowing God, they lift not hands of prayer,
>   Both for themselves and those who call them friend?
>   For so the whole round world is every way
>   Bound by gold chains about the feet of God."

I do not suspect there is a creature here who never
prays because people generally pray to somebody or other. The man that never prays to God such prayers as he

ought, prays to God such prayers as he ought not! It is an awful thing when a man asks God to damn him—and yet there are persons that do that! Suppose He were to hear you? He is a prayer-hearing God!

If I address one profane swearer here I would like to put this matter clearly to him. Were the Almighty to hear you—if your eyes were blinded and your tongue were struck dumb while you were uttering a wild impreca-tion—how would you bear the sudden judgment on your impious speech? If some of those prayers of yours were answered for yourself—and if some that you have offered in your passion for your wife and for your child were ful-filled to their hurt and your distraction—what an awful thing it would be!

Well, God does answer prayer, and one of these days He may answer your prayers to your shame and everlast-ing confusion. Would not it be well now, before you leave your seat, to pray, "Lord, have mercy upon me. Lord, save me. Lord, change my heart. Lord, give me to believe in Christ. Lord, give me now an interest in the precious blood of Jesus. Lord, save me now"? Will not each one of you breathe such a prayer as that? May the Holy Spirit lead you to do so! And if you once begin to pray aright I am not afraid that you will never leave off, for there is a some-thing that holds the soul fast in real prayer.

Made in the USA
Columbia, SC
20 March 2020